raising the heat

WARM STEAK SALAD

PAUL GAYLER

cooking with fire and spice

photography by Gus Filgate

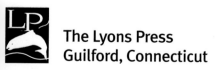

The Lyons Press
Guilford, Connecticut

An imprint of The Globe Pequot Press

raising the heat

To my wife Anita and children – with love

First Lyons Press edition, 2001

First published in Great Britain in 2000 by Kyle Cathie Limited

Text copyright © 2000 by Paul Gayler
Photography copyright © 2000 by Gus Filgate

The Lyons Press is an imprint of The Globe Pequot Press.

Printed and bound in Singapore

ISBN 1-58574-462-X

10 9 8 7 6 5 4 3 2 1

The Library of Congress Cataloguing-in-Publication Data is available on file.

contents

Introduction

I grew up in the East End of London at a time when fish and chips and jellied eels were the norm. My father ran a café for a while, which became a Chinese restaurant after he sold it. I took the opportunity of working there for a brief period while I was at college and the food made a lasting impression on me. It was my first encounter with spices and exotic flavorings. Chinese cooks use spices as much for their fragrance as for their heat, particularly star anise, ginger, garlic, and sesame. Later, as a chef, I followed the usual classical French path but I also made a point of working in Indian restaurants, where I was amazed by the beguiling array of spices, with their jewel-like shades of ruby red, glowing orange, and deep ochre. In Indian cooking, as many as a dozen spices may be blended together to flavor one dish. On a working visit to Singapore and Malaysia, I learned that chiles and other fiery ingredients were valuable not only for their heat but for their subtle, complex flavors. In Southeast Asia, the heat is tempered by cooling ingredients, such as coconut milk, lime juice, and lemongrass, to produce an aromatic, perfectly balanced cuisine.

In 1990 I joined the Lanesborough and became acquainted with an entirely different style of spicing – that of the American Southwest, which borrows heavily from Mexican cooking. The Lanesborough belongs to the same group as the Mansion on Turtle Creek in Dallas, one of the world's top hotels. Its head chef, Dean Fearing, is a leading exponent of Southwestern cuisine. Based on corn, beans, squashes, spices and chiles, with a plentiful supply of good meat and seafood, this is full of vigorous, sun-drenched flavors. Hearty stews are fired up with spices and dried chiles (chile con carne is a Southwestern dish rather than a Mexican one), while simple roasts and grills are served with spicy relishes and barbecue sauces. What started as cowboy cooking is becoming increasingly refined under chefs like Dean, yet nothing prepared me for the subtleties of genuine Mexican cooking, which I experienced when Alicia De'Angeli of the El Tajin restaurant in Mexico City visited the Lanesborough with a team of chefs for a promotion on Mexican food. They taught me about the intricacies of using dried chiles and layering flavors. Mexican cuisine is not necessarily hot. The piquancy can easily be controlled, and chiles add interest and flavor, not just fire.

Besides Oriental flavors, I have also learned to love the warm spices of North Africa and the Mediterranean (cumin, saffron, cinnamon, coriander, paprika) and the vibrant cooking of the Caribbean, which combines palate-singeing chiles with wonderful tropical fruits and vegetables. Over the years, my fascination with hot foods has remained undimmed. I would rather eat a curry or a Chinese meal than just about anything else, and I am not alone in this. Once people start to eat spicy food they tend to get hooked. The scientific explanation is that the sensation of pain when you consume chiles and other hot spices releases endorphins in the body, which cause a "high." This pain/pleasure equation means that some chili addicts think the hotter the better. Personally, I believe there's more to spicy food than a blast of heat, stimulating though that can be. It is not until you explore the full range of chiles that you realize how complex the underlying flavors are, and that these, too, make a vital contribution. The pasilla, for example, a favourite chili in Mexico and America's Southwest, has a rich, raisiny, almost chocolatey taste, while the mighty habanero has a fruity flavor and the heat of the jalapeño is offset by sweetness.

Although chiles reign supreme in the world of hot foods, they are not the only way of adding fire to your cooking. Other spicy ingredients include, mustard, horseradish, ginger, peppercorns and some greens, such as arugula, mizuna and the curry leaf. Even sausages, such as the Spanish chorizo and the North African merguez, have a role to play. Mustard, horseradish, and pepper can rival chiles in heat, while ginger has a slow burn that refreshes and warms at the same time. Greens tend to be only mildly spicy, useful for pepping up a salad or vegetable dish. Very often it is the combination of flavorings that provides a dish's heat – something Oriental cooks understand well, with their unique spice blends such as the Chinese five-spice powder and the Indian garam masalas.

Raising the Heat is something of a whirlwind tour around the spicy cuisines of the world. You may find your head begins to spin as you turn from an incendiary South Indian curry to a sizzling-hot Szechuan-style stir-fry, then to a classic Italian pasta *arrabbiata* or Mexican *mole*. But the exhilarating thing about hot foods is that there are no restrictions – they can be enjoyed within the context of just about any nation's cooking (even we British have our horseradish sauce and hot mustards). Although I have included some classics, I don't claim that all these recipes are authentic (anyway it's virtually impossible to reproduce another country's dishes accurately – better to develop them to suit the produce available). In fact, I am a bit of a culinary floozie in this respect. As a hot-food addict, I have picked up ideas for spicy dishes on my travels around the world but I find it impossible to be faithful to any one type of cooking. I love combining a Cajun technique, say, with Asian spices to create a new fish dish, or a Mexican sauce with an Eastern-style treatment for meat or poultry. My cooking has always tended towards this sort of culinary promiscuity, but recently, combining flavors and techniques from different cuisines has become fashionable and earned itself a label – fusion food.

Fusion food first took off in America and Australia, where you can find some of the most exciting and intelligent examples of the trend. All too often, though, fusion can lead to confusion – throwing ingredients together just for novelty's sake doesn't work. To put a new spin on old favorites, it's essential to learn the basics first and to understand how flavors work together. Then you can open your mind to new ideas. As far as spicy foods go, this means showing some restraint. Try to balance the flavors and textures of each dish, and don't choose an entire menu of chili-hot dishes. Contrast is important. In hot countries, where most spicy food originates (because, curiously enough, hot food cools you down), this is often done by combining a hot dish with a cooling relish – think of the yogurt raita of India, the mint labna of the Middle East, and the fruity salsas of Mexico.

You may notice that there are a lot of recipes for seafood in this book. This is partly because people are eating more fish now but also because I find it has a real affinity with spices – not just robust fish, such as tuna and mackerel, but more delicate ones like sole and cod. Seafood such as lobster and scallops is usually given a classical treatment but its firm, sweet flesh makes the perfect partner for chiles and other hot ingredients – try Goan red masala lobster (page 66), or Grilled scallops with black bean and citrus chili oil vinaigrette (page 35), if you remain unconvinced.

If you are fairly new to spicy food, there are plenty of mild dishes in this book that you can make in order to acclimate yourself before working up to the really hot stuff. Try the Celeriac and mustard soup (page 15), for example, or the Cioppino (page 64) to experience a gentle warming glow rather than blazing heat. If you are a real chile aficionado, on the other hand, you may want to plunge straight into Fiery Keralan chicken (page 74) or Prawns piri-piri (page 65). Whatever your preference, you can control the heat level yourself by the amount of spicing you add. If in any doubt about the chile tolerance of your guests, season your main dishes cautiously but serve them with fiery condiments or relishes (see Sauces and spices mixes on pages 142–157), so that they can spice their own food.

You won't need any special equipment for the recipes in this book but it is essential to have a powerful blender or food processor for making spice pastes and sauces. A spice grinder is also useful but a coffee mill or mortar and pestle, will do instead. Although some of the ingredients may seem unfamiliar, it's surprising what you can buy at large supermarkets nowadays, while most big cities have Asian or Chinese food shops, which are an invaluable source of reasonably priced spices and fresh herbs. More and more shops supply by mail order now, or over the Internet.

I hope the recipes in this book will set both your imagination and palate alight. Raise the heat in your cooking and explore the full range of fiery flavors from around the world.

All recipes serve 4 unless otherwise stated. ✳ indicates extra hot dishes.

The hot store cupboard – a guide to hot and spicy ingredients

Chiles – the ultimate heat

Chile is the common name given to the fruit of a type of capsicum, grown all over the world but particularly in countries with a spicy cuisine, such as Mexico, India, and the Caribbean. There are at least 200 varieties, varying from mild to searingly hot, and they come in a range of colors, shapes, and sizes. They all share the same pod-like construction, however, with a central cavity containing small white seeds. The seeds and ribs contain most of the chile's capsaicin, the volatile oil that is the source of its heat.

Fresh chiles are green until they ripen, when they turn red or, in some cases, yellow, orange, purple, or black. Some varieties are sold both ripe and unripe. Ripe chiles can be just as fiery as green ones but they tend to have a sweeter, more distinct vegetable flavor. In general, the larger the chile, the milder it is, but this cannot be absolutely relied upon; even chiles from the same plant can vary greatly in strength. The best varieties are arguably produced in the West, although I'm sure the Asians would have something to say on that score. Certainly the most fragrant chiles come from South America. Once chiles are dried, their potency increases and their flavor becomes more complex, aided by a huge concentration of natural sugars. Their depth of flavor makes them an invaluable addition to sauces and slow-cooked braises and stews. As a rough rule of thumb, dried chiles can be divided into two categories – small hot ones and large mild ones – although, as with fresh chiles, there are lots of exceptions. Below is a guide to the chiles used in this book, with a rating out of ten to give an indication of their heat. Remember, though, that the only way of knowing for sure how hot an individual chile is is to taste it. In Mexico, they bite into them before use.

Buying and Storing Chiles

Fresh With more and more varieties available from mail order and specialist shops, finding the right chile is not generally a problem. Even in supermarkets you may find individual types labeled by name. More often, however, there will just be one or two anonymous varieties – these are probably Lombok or some form of Cayenne. Whatever sort of chile you buy, make sure they are firm, shiny, and unwrinkled, without any soft spots. They will keep in the fridge for up to 3 weeks if thoroughly wrapped in paper towel. Do not store them in plastic bags as the moisture created will cause them to shrivel. Left out in the air, they tend to wrinkle and lose flavor.

Dried When buying dried chiles, choose ones that are uniform in shape and avoid any that are faded or dusty. They should have a good aroma and, although dried, they should have some degree of flexibility, indicating freshness. Do not buy too many dried chiles at once; to enjoy them at their best they should be used within three months of purchase. Store in an airtight container to preserve their fragrant qualities.

Preparing Chiles

Chiles can literally burn, and should be handled with care. The capsaicin, which is concentrated in the ribs and seeds, and present in smaller quantities in the flesh, is the culprit. If you have any cuts on your hands, or if you rub your eyes after preparing chiles, the pain can be excruciating. For protection, I suggest you wear thin rubber gloves, which can be thrown away afterwards. Thin-skinned chiles have the highest level of capsaicin.

Some recipes in this book call for chiles to be seeded, while in others the seeds are left in. This is a way of controlling the heat; if the chiles are too hot for your taste, then remove the seeds – and cut off the ribs as well if you like. You will still be left with all the flavor, which is in the flesh. With dried chiles the capsaicin is spread throughout the chile, so seeding them doesn't make much difference to the degree of heat. When a recipe specifies chopped chiles, simply remove the stem end, cut the chile in half down the center, and then use a small knife to scrape out the seeds, if you wish. Cut the chile into small dice with a sharp knife or scissors. Always wash your hands in hot soapy water before continuing with the recipe.

Large fresh chiles such as the poblano and New Mexican have tough skins, so it is common to roast and peel them before use (see below).

Roasting Fresh Chiles Roasting brings out the full flavor of fresh chiles and fills the air with a matchless fragrance. Simply place the chiles directly over a gas flame and leave for about 2–3 minutes, turning with tongs occasionally, until they are blistered and blackened all over. If you don't have a gas stove, broil about 2 inches away from the heat, turning frequently, until charred. Or you can roast them in an oven preheated to 400°F for 5–6 minutes, drizzled with a little olive oil. When the chiles are ready, place them in a plastic bag, tie to seal it, and set aside for 10–15 minutes; the steam created will help loosen the skins. Rinse the chiles under cold water, peel off the skins with a small knife, and then use as needed.

Roasting Dried Chiles In South American countries, dried chiles are usually roasted and then rehydrated in hot water before use. Remove the stem from the chiles and shake out the seeds, then place the chiles on a baking sheet and roast for 2–3 minutes in an oven preheated to 375°F. Otherwise, place under the broiler on low heat. Take great care not to burn or scorch the chiles, or they will taste bitter.

Putting Out the Fire

If your mouth is left burning after eating hot chiles, don't drink water or beer, which will only spread the capsaicin further and make things worse. Instead, try dairy products, such as milk, cheese, yoghurt, or ice cream, which will help neutralize the heat. I know people who swear by eating bread, or even a spoonful of sugar.

Fresh Chiles

Bird's Eye (8/10) These tiny, explosive chiles are used in Thai cooking and can be green, orange, or red. They are very similar to Thai chiles (see below).

Habanero (10/10) Sometimes confused with the Scotch bonnet, this is probably the hottest chile available, said to be 75 times hotter than the jalapeño, so beware! The habanero is lantern shaped, measuring about 2 inches long and 1½ inches wide, and comes in all colors, although yellow and red are the most common. Despite its intense heat, the habanero has a fruity tone that goes particularly well with dishes containing tropical fruits and tomatoes. It is generally seeded and used very sparingly in salsas, sauces, stews, and marinades. So fierce is this chile that it can irritate the skin, so take great care when handling.

Hungarian Cherry Chile Pepper (3/10) This round, thick, fleshy chile contains a lot of seeds. It is quite sweet when ripe, with a medium heat. Use in soups or salads, or stuff with a meat or cheese filling, and bake.

Hungarian Hot Wax (4/10) This large, long, slightly twisted chile starts yellow and matures to an orange-red color. It can grow up to 5 inches in length and is generally used for frying, in spicy salads, or for dressings.

Jalapeño (5/10) A shiny, torpedo-shaped, bright-green chile from the state of Veracruz in Mexico. Measuring 2–3 inches in length, it was originally very hot, although it now seems to vary and can be fairly mild. It is the most common chile in the United States and is great for making spicy salsas, dips, and pizza toppings, or as a flavoring for cornbread (see page 136). The jalapeño is also sold ripe and red, when it is slightly sweeter and less hot.

Lombok (3/10) These long, thin chiles originate from Indonesia but are now the commonest variety found in big stores and supermarkets, sometimes simply labeled mild chiles. Use in soups, salsas, and stir-fries.

New Mexican (5/10) This moderately hot, elongated chile is sometimes known as the long green chile. It is used in sauces, stews, and salsas and, like the poblano, can be stuffed to make the classic Mexican dish, *chiles rellenos*. It is wonderful roasted, which brings out its sweet, rather fruity flavor.

Poblano (3/10) This impressive-looking chile, has a purple-black tinge to its dark green flesh and resembles a green pepper in appearance and in size, but tapers down from the shoulders to a point. It is usually mild. Poblanos are always roasted and peeled before use, as they have a tough skin that is not easily digestible. Roasting gives them a smoky, even earthy flavor. They are used in sauces, especially Mexican *mole* sauces, or stuffed to make *chiles rellenos*, then dipped in batter and deep-fried. When

dried, the poblano is known as the ancho chile (see below).

Serrano (7/10) This small chile has a lively heat and is available both unripened (green) and ripe (red), although red is more common. It is generally used in salsas and in the classic Mexican guacamole. You can also roast it and use in sauces to give them a little more bite. It is also available pickled.

Thai (8/10) Also known as the Japanese or Asian chile, this is small and narrow and can be red or green in color. It has meaty flesh, with a high proportion of seeds and an intriguing, lingering heat. Use sparingly unless you have a high chile tolerance. Thai chiles are good added whole to Thai-style curries and stir-fries. If they are not available, substitute two serrano chiles for each Thai chile. They are at their freshest when sold in small clusters.

Dried Chiles

Ancho (4/10) The ancho is a dried poblano chile that has become wrinkled and deep red. It measures 4–5 inches in length and 3 inches wide across the top (*ancho* means wide in Spanish). It is the fruitiest and sweetest of the dried chiles, rich yet mild in flavor, and is generally soaked and puréed to make Mexican-style sauces and *moles*.

Cascabel (4/10) The cascabel derives its name from the Spanish for rattle, the sound given off by the seeds when these little round chiles are shaken. They have a smoky, slightly acidic flavor. Sauces, stews, and salsas all benefit from their nutty, assertive taste.

Chipotle (7/10) This is a dried smoked jalapeño, with a deep, well-rounded heat and a smoky-sweet, chocolatey flavor. It is generally used in sauces, soups, and salsas, but is good in almost anything. Chipotles are also available canned in red adobo sauce.

De Arbol (8/10) This long, red-black, pointed chile is fiery yet grassy in flavor, with a searing heat. Use in sauces and soups and for making chili oil. It is widely available in powdered form and is also available fresh, when it is small and green.

Guajillo (4/10) A long, tender, thin-fleshed chile with a deep orange color. It is moderately hot and has a slightly tangy, fruity taste with a green tea overtone.

The guajillo is often combined with other varieties to give dishes a distinct flavor and orange tint.

New Mexican Red (4/10) A bright-scarlet, thin-fleshed chile with a sweet, cherry-like flavor, this has a smooth, crisp, and clean heat. It is indispensable for making red chile sauce and is also sold powdered or in flakes. It is thought by many to be the doyenne of chiles – quite a reputation to live up to!

Pasilla (4/10) Sometimes known as the chile negro (black chile), this tastes like dried raisins but with a slightly herby overtone. It has a medium heat and is great in Mexican mole sauces, with seafood, or sautéed with woodland mushrooms.

Peperoncino (6/10) An orange-red Italian chile with a hot, sweet flavor. It is commonly used in tomato-based dishes and is also good with seafood.

Chili Powders

Cayenne Pepper Originally from the Cayenne region of French Guyana, this is ground from the dried, small, hot chile of the same name. It is very pungent, with a sharp bite, so use sparingly.

Chili Powder This is the most readily obtainable form of chile. However, I find it gives heat but no real flavor, as it is usually blended with other ingredients such as herbs and spices which detract from the taste. Use only in an emergency. Otherwise, you can make your own very easily by roasting dried chiles (see page 8), then grinding them in a spice mill or coffee grinder. Store in jars or airtight bags. The advantage of making chili powder yourself is that you can use whatever type of chile you prefer, or a combination. My favorite for this purpose is the New Mexican Red.

Dried Chili Flakes These are simply crushed dried chiles, including the seeds. They are useful for pepping up all manner of dishes, including pasta sauces and pizzas. Dried red chili flakes are the most common but you might also be able to find crushed green jalapeño flakes, which have a sweet yet fiery flavor.

Paprika Paprika is ground from a dried sweet red pepper, the *Capsicum annum*. There are two types: hot paprika, from Hungary, which is almost as fierce as cayenne, and mild (sweet) paprika from Spain, which has a wonderful smoky flavor. Both are used in soups, stews (such as the Hungarian *gulyás*, or goulash), and sausages.

Chile Sauces, Pastes and Condiments

Chili Jelly Popular in Southwest American cooking, this spicy-sweet jelly (see page 148) is wonderful for glazing meat or can be served as a relish – it is particularly good with duck.

Chili Oil Widely used in oriental cooking, this is made by steeping hot chiles in a bland oil such as peanut. It is used as a condiment, in dressings, or added to dishes after cooking. You will find a recipe for chili oil and some interesting variations on page 152.

Harissa Reasonable versions of this North African chili paste can be bought in tubes or tins. To experience it at its best, though, it's worth making your own (see page 156).

Hot Pepper Sauce A thin, red, West Indian sauce made from habanero chiles, with enough bite to flavor anything. Use sparingly in sauces and salsas.

Mexican Chile Sauce This is a fiery, thin, red sauce, used to flavor meat for enchiladas and other Mexican dishes. The commercial product tends to be a poor substitute for the real thing (see recipe on page 146), although it is useful to have in stock for emergencies.

Mexican Salsas Mexican salsas are simple chunky relishes made from finely chopped fresh ingredients such as tomatoes, onions, or even fruit, spiked with chile and herbs. This is one area where there really is no substitute for making your own. Most salsas are very simple to prepare, with little or no cooking involved – it's just a question of chopping your ingredients and letting them marinate for a short while. (Try the recipes on pages 150–151).

Sambal In Southeast Asia, especially Indonesia, there is a whole family of sambals – pungent pastes served in small quantities for dipping. They are available from most Asian stores, or try the recipe on page 148.

Spicy Bean Sauce A dark, pungent, Chinese seasoning paste made from black beans, garlic, ginger, soy sauce, and lots of chile. Look for a good-quality commercial product and use it to enliven sauces and stir-fries, especially if you like your food hot. Or mix with sweet chile sauce to make a condiment.

Sweet Chile Sauce Used in Asian cookery, this is just as it sounds – a spicy yet sweet-tasting sauce, great for stir-fries, sauces, and dressings. It's easy to buy but almost as easy to make – try the recipe on page 147.

Tabasco Sauce A ferociously hot, thin, almost citric liquid, made in Louisiana from puréed cayenne chiles and vinegar. It gives a wonderful kick to soups and sauces. I am a member of the Tabasco Club, an informal association of Tabasco lovers, which was formed in appreciation of this addictive ingredient.

Spice mixes

Cajun Spice Mix Used in Creole and Cajun cooking in America's Deep South, this is a punchy blend of chile, spices, dried herbs, and garlic (see the recipe on page 157). It is generally rubbed over fish or meat before grilling or roasting .

Chinese Five-spice Powder A fragrant blend of cinnamon, star anise, Szechuan pepper, cloves, and fennel seeds, this is now available in most supermarkets. Use for spicing up meat and fish. It is particularly good for marinades and slow-cooked dishes.

Curry Powders and Pastes Curry is not an Indian word at all, but a term the British Colonials applied to all Indian spice blends. Jars of curry powder or paste can be bought ready-made, but in India no such spice mix is recognized, since cooks always prepare their own fragrant blends. These vary from region to region, and according to personal taste and what dish it is being used for. Bought curry powder or paste is a convenient stand-by but once opened, it quickly becomes stale. It doesn't take very long to make your own and it will pay dividends in terms of flavor. I have included several of my favorite curry powders and spice mixes in this book (see pages 156–157).

Garam Masala Garam masala means 'hot spices' and is a mixture of cinnamon, cardamom, cloves, cumin, black pepper, and other spices according to taste. It is generally added to dishes at the last moment to liven up the flavors. Commercial versions rapidly deteriorate in flavor, so it is a good idea to mix up your own – preferably using freshly ground spices (page 66).

Indian Five-Spice Powder This aromatic spice mix is not as well known as the Chinese five-spice powder. It consists of equal measures of ground cumin, black mustard, fenugreek, fennel, and nigella seeds. It is not always sold as a mix, so if you cannot find it, buy the seeds whole and grind them yourself – even better!

Other hot spices

Galangal

Widely used in Southeast Asian cooking, this rhizome is related to ginger and has a similar flavor, although more citrusy. There are two varieties, greater and lesser galangal, and it is the lesser that has the stronger flavor. Use in the same way as ginger, which can be substituted if galangal is unavailable.

Ginger

This knobbly, aromatic rhizome is an essential ingredient in Asian cooking and is popular the world over. It has a light brown skin, which is always peeled off before use, and juicy, pale yellow flesh, with a sharp refreshing flavor. Store, tightly wrapped, in the refrigerator, where it will keep for several weeks.

Pickled Pink Ginger A staple of Japanese cooking, this ingredient is made by preserving paper-thin slices of young ginger root in a vinegar solution. It is traditionally used as a seasoning or condiment for sushi and sashimi.

Mustard

Mustard is the name given to the seeds of the yellow, black, or brown mustard plant, the black being the hottest. Mixed with wine or vinegar and seasonings, it is a favorite spice the world over, although styles vary according to country. The Chinese, for example, prefer hot mustard, the Scandinavians sweet mustard. The texture can be smooth or coarse, and flavorings such as tarragon or honey are often added.

Dijon Mustard This is a smooth, pale-yellow, clean-tasting mustard made from black or brown seeds blended with verjuice (unripe grape juice), salt, and spices. It is usually quite mild, although it can vary in strength. Dijon mustard is used in classic French-style sauces and salad dressings.

English Mustard English mustard is sharp and slightly acidic in flavor, and is available as a powder or made into a paste. Traditionally it is served as an accompaniment to roast beef and other meats.

Grain Mustard To make grain mustard the seeds are partly crushed and partly ground, to give a crunchy texture, then mixed with spices, vinegar, and sometimes other flavorings, too. It is usually medium hot and is good served with cold meats and sausages. Meaux mustard is a favorite of mine and I am also very fond of the green peppercorn variety.

Mustard Oil This is used in India in the same way as ghee, and is available from Indian and Asian grocers. It is golden brown and extremely pungent, and may be sold pure or blended with other oils. Mustard oil is also used in commercial salad dressings and in the Italian *mostarda di Cremona*, or *mostarda di frutta* (mixed candied fruits in mustard syrup).

Mustard Seeds Black mustard seeds are widely used in Indian cooking, both whole and ground. The whole seeds are usually dry-roasted first to extract the fragrance. Most mustard is made from brown mustard seeds, while yellow seeds are used for mild American mustards and for pickling.

Pepper

Sometimes known as the king of spices, the peppercorn is the fruit of the vine pepper, *Piper nigrum*. Each variety has a different aroma and taste, all with the underlying heat of basic black pepper.

Black Peppercorns The familiar black peppercorn is picked while green and then left to dry, when it wrinkles and blackens. It is very pungent and fiery.

Green Peppercorns These are unripe fresh peppercorns, preserved by bottling in brine or vinegar or, more recently, by freeze-drying. It is milder in flavor than black pepper, with a clean, fresh taste.

Mignonette Pepper Widely used in France, this is a rough mixture of cracked black and white peppercorns.

Pink Peppercorns This is not a peppercorn at all but an aromatic berry native to South America. Available dried or bottled in vinegar, it has a brittle, slightly bitter skin. I find the bottled variety has a better flavor.

Sansho Also called Japanese pepper, this is the ground dried leaves of the tree that produces Szechuan pepper but its character is entirely different. It has a citrus fragrance with a hint of lychee and a mild, peppery taste. Look for it in Japanese shops.

Szechuan Pepper Like pink pepper, this is not a member of the peppercorn family but a dried berry. It comes from a small tree, native to China, and has a spicy, peppery flavor. It is used throughout Asia but particularly in Chinese cooking. Szechuan peppercorns are normally roasted before use to bring out their wonderful flavor. You should be able to find them in Chinese shops or large supermarkets. If necessary, freshly ground black pepper can be substituted.

White Peppercorns These are picked when ripe, then soaked in water to remove the outer coating, and dried. They are hotter and less fragrant than black pepper.

Wasabi

Also known as Japanese horseradish, wasabi is a fierce, heady condiment available in powder or paste form. When mixed with water, it is much stronger than fresh horseradish. It is widely used in Japanese cooking, particularly in sushi.

Spicy ingredients

Horseradish

Horseradish is a large, knarled white root. Fresh horseradish, usually available in early spring, must be peeled and grated before use but it gives off such powerful vapors that this task can bring tears to the eyes. However, it's worth persevering, as the flavor is incomparable. It is also available ready grated in jars, which makes a reasonable substitute, or dried and powdered. Try to avoid ready-made horseradish sauces, which are generally full of unnecessary additives.

Leaves

Arugula Arugula tends to be considered as a salad green but in Italy this peppery plant has always been used in cooking, too, particularly in pasta sauces and soups. It also makes a fine pesto. Wild arugula has a more assertive taste than the cultivated variety.

Curry Leaves These are not related to curry powder. Used in South Indian cooking, they are the small, almond-shaped leaves of the curry plant, and have a warm, spicy flavor. Asian shops sell dried curry leaves and occasionally fresh ones, which are much better. If you can find only dried curry leaves you will need to use at least twice as many, since the flavor is weaker. Fresh leaves will keep in the fridge for a week or so.

Mustard Leaves The mustard plant is a prized vegetable throughout India and is fast becoming a fashionable salad green in the West. Of the several varieties available I think mizuna is the best. It has green leaves with a ragged edge and a slightly spicy flavor.

Nasturtium Leaves Nasturtiums grow in many people's gardens but few realise that they make a delightful addition to soups and salads, too. They have a pungent flavor and aroma, reminiscent of caper berries, and should be used with discretion. The leaves (and flowers, which have a peppery taste) make an interesting addition to sandwiches and are also good with cheese dishes.

Watercress An aquatic member of the mustard family, this has a vigorous, peppery flavor. Too often relegated to the role of garnish, it makes excellent purées, sauces, and soups.

Radishes

Radishes were first cultivated in China, Japan, and India but they are now found in all temperate regions of Europe. There are a great many varieties – round, long, pink, black, white, green, and purple. They are normally eaten raw but the leaves of pink radishes can also be cooked like spinach.

Sausages

Using spicy sausages in cooking is an easy way of adding fire to your food. Here are some of my favorites:

Andouille Not to be confused with the milder French sausage of the same name, this spicy, heavily smoked pork sausage is a specialty of Louisiana. It is an essential ingredient in jambalaya, gumbo, and other Cajun dishes.

Chorizo This Spanish pork sausage contains paprika, which gives it both its heat and its color. Available both smoked and unsmoked, it is used in both Spanish and Mexican cooking.

Kielbasa This is a spicy boiling sausage from Poland, made of beef and pork, garlic, and black pepper.

Merguez Full of North African spicing, this lamb sausage can be searingly hot. It originates from Algeria but is now used throughout North Africa and is popular in France, too.

Peperoni A coarse sausage from Italy, flavored with fennel, spices, and chile.

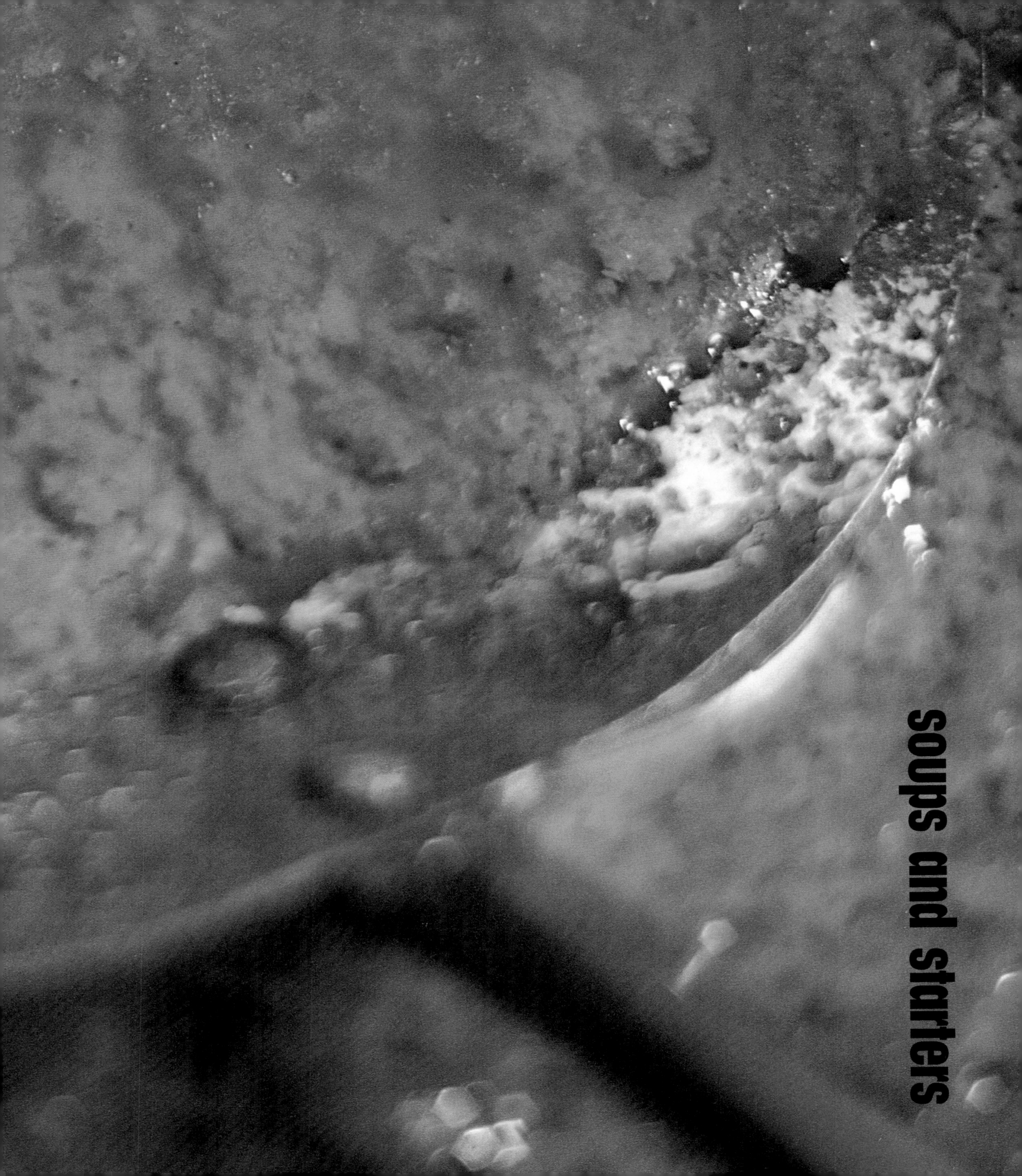

soups and starters

Thai-inspired pumpkin and basil soup

If you can find Thai basil, which is sometimes available from Asian grocery stores, the soup will have a more authentic flavor. But it's delicious made with ordinary basil, too.

Heat the butter in a very large frying pan or a pot, add the diced pumpkin and fry for 3–4 minutes, until colored. Add the onion, garlic, galangal or ginger, and chile, and cook for 2 minutes. Stir in the paste and cook for 1 minute, until fragrant. Add the chicken stock and bring to a boil, then reduce the heat and simmer until the pumpkin is just tender. Finally, stir in the coconut milk and torn basil leaves, and season to taste.

Serve immediately in 4 individual bowls.

2 tablespoons sweet butter
1lb. pumpkin or butternut squash,
  peeled and cut into 1/2 inch dice
1 onion, chopped
2 garlic cloves, crushed
1 teaspoon finely chopped fresh galangal
  or ginger
1 Thai chile, thinly sliced
1 tablespoon Red Thai Curry Paste
  (see p.155)
1 quart chicken stock
3/4 cup coconut milk
8 basil leaves, torn into small pieces
Salt and freshly ground black pepper

Celeriac and mustard soup

Back in 1979 I was asked to prepare an eight-course vegetarian dinner for 250 people for a diamond company in Antwerp, Belgium. The meal was a great success and I brought the recipe for this soup back from Antwerp. It is beautifully creamy with just a little mustard bite.

Melt the butter in a large pot, add the leek, then cover and cook over low heat for about 5 minutes, until soft. Add the diced celeriac and potatoes, and sweat for 5 minutes. Stir in 1 tablespoon of the mustard and the chicken stock, bring to a boil, then reduce the heat and simmer until the vegetables are tender. Place in a blender and blitz until smooth.

Return the soup to a clean pot, stir in the heavy cream and the remaining mustard, and reheat gently. Sprinkle with the chopped chives before serving.

2 tablespoons sweet butter
1 small leek, chopped
1 medium-sized celeriac, peeled and chopped
2 potatoes, peeled and chopped
2 tablespoons Dijon mustard
1 quart well-flavored chicken stock
2/3 cup heavy cream
1 tablespoon chopped chives

Black bean and squid ink soup

If you prefer, you could blitz this soup to a smooth purée rather than leaving it rough-textured. Either way, it's a wonderful warming bowlful.

Place the soaked beans in a large pot, cover with water, and bring to a boil. Drain the beans in a colander and then return to the pot. Add the chicken stock or water and bring to a boil, then add the garlic and thyme and reduce the heat to a simmer. Cook for 1–11/2 hours, then stir in the vegetables and jalapeño chiles and simmer for 30 minutes, until everything is tender.

Place the mixture in a blender and blitz to a coarse texture. Return to a clean pot and bring back to a boil. Season to taste, stir in the squid ink and lemon juice, and keep warm.

Gently heat the chili oil in a frying pan, season the squid with salt and pepper, and fry quickly for 1 minute. Serve in individual bowls, topped with the sautéed squid, and sprinkled with the cilantro.

HOT TIP Squid ink is available in small sachets from some fishmarkets.

Serves 4–6
3/4 cup black beans, soaked overnight and then drained
5 cups chicken stock or water
1 garlic clove, chopped
1 teaspoon fresh thyme
1 carrot, finely diced
1 onion, finely diced
2 celery stalks, finely diced
1 red pepper, roasted, peeled, and finely diced
2 green jalapeño chiles, seeded and finely diced
2 tablespoons squid ink
Juice of 1/2 lemon
1/4 cup Chili Oil (see page 152)
5 ounces baby squid, cleaned and cut into rings
2 tablespoons chopped cilantro
Salt and freshly ground black pepper

Chilled smoky tomato soup
with paprika sour cream

Preheat the broiler to its highest setting. Put the tomatoes in a bowl and toss them with half the olive oil, then place on the broiler rack. Place under the hot broiler for 8–10 minutes or until they are soft and slightly charred.

Heat the remaining oil in a large pot, add the onion, garlic, cumin, coriander, and half the paprika, and fry gently until softened but not colored. Add the cherry chile peppers, followed by the charred tomatoes and the tomato paste, and cook over low heat for 5 minutes. Pour in the chicken stock and bring to a boil, then reduce the heat and simmer for 2 minutes. Pour the soup through a fine strainer. Add the vinegar and sugar, return the soup to the pot, bring to a boil, and simmer for 3–5 minutes. Remove from the heat, let cool, and then chill. Season with salt and pepper when cold.

To serve, ladle into individual soup bowls. Blend together the sour cream and the remaining paprika, top each bowlful with a dollop of cream, and sprinkle on a little extra paprika. Stir in gently to create a decorative swirl.

HOT TIP Don't purée this soup in a blender – it tends to lose its color and becomes a washed-out shade of pink.

31/2 lbs. ripe but firm plum tomatoes, cut in half

1/4 cup olive oil

1 onion, chopped

2 garlic cloves, crushed

2 teaspoons ground cumin

1/2 teaspoon ground coriander

2 teaspoons smoked paprika, plus extra for garnishing

2 Hungarian cherry chile peppers, seeded and chopped

1 tablespoon tomato paste

1 quart chicken stock

1/4 cup balsamic vinegar

11/2 tablespoons sugar

1/4 cup sour cream

Salt and freshly ground black pepper

Romaine lettuce and nasturtium soup

Nasturtium leaves add a delicate, peppery flavor to this simple summer soup, which can also be served chilled. If you can't find any nasturtiums, they are very easy to grow, with the added bonus that the flowers can be used to garnish salads.

Wash and shred the lettuce and nasturtium leaves. Melt the butter in a pot, add the onion and leek and sweat for 4–5 minutes, until softened. Add the shredded lettuce and nasturtium leaves, then pour in the stock, season with a little salt, and bring to a boil. Add the potatoes, reduce the heat, and simmer until the potatoes are tender.

Place in a blender and blitz to a smooth purée. Return to the pot, add the cream, and simmer for 2–3 minutes. Add a pinch of sugar and season.

Pour into individual serving bowls and garnish with shredded nasturtium leaves.

14 ounces romaine lettuce

1 ounce fresh nasturtium leaves, plus extra for garnishing

2 tablespoons sweet butter

1 onion, roughly chopped

1 leek, chopped

3 cups well-flavored chicken stock

1 cup potatoes, peeled and chopped

2/3 cup light cream or milk

A pinch of sugar

Salt and freshly ground black pepper

CHILLED SMOKY TOMATO SOUP

Arepa soup
(creamed green chile polenta soup with shellfish)

This is an adaptation of a soup I had in one of America's best-loved Mexican restaurants.

Scrub the mussels and clams under cold running water, de-bearding the mussels and discarding any open ones that don't close when tapped on a work surface. Place the mussels and clams in a large pot, along with the shallots and half the chile, pour in the white wine and chicken stock, then cover the pot and cook over high heat for 3–4 minutes, shaking the pot occasionally, until the shells open. Drain the mussels and clams in a colander, then strain the cooking liquor into a clean pot. Bring to a boil, and add the milk. Rain in the polenta and cook over low heat, stirring constantly, for 4–5 minutes or until thickened.

Remove the mussels and clams from their shells. Place the polenta soup in a blender, add half the mussels and clams and half the corn, and blitz to a smooth purée.

Return to the pot, add the cream and bring to a boil. Season to taste, then add the remaining mussels, clams, and corn, together with the shrimp.

Serve garnished with the remaining chile.

2 1/4 lbs. mussels

1lb., 2oz. clams

2 shallots, finely sliced

2 green chiles, finely sliced

1/2 cup dry white wine

1 quart chicken stock

2/3 cup whole milk

1 cup polenta (cornmeal)

1 1/4 cups cooked corn

1/2 cup heavy cream

3/4 cups small Norwegian shrimp

Salt and freshly ground black pepper

Caldo de albóndigas

This is a classic Mexican soup of spicy meatballs cooked in chicken broth. I find a lot of chicken broths tasteless, with no depth or body. Here is an exception to the rule – a broth that is bursting with flavor. It is traditionally served with Spanish-style meatballs and accompanied by a smoky guacamole.

First prepare the meatballs by mixing all the ingredients together in a bowl. Season with salt and pepper, then, using your hands, shape the mixture into 20 small meatballs.

With a knife, remove the corn kernels from the cob. Bring the chicken stock to a boil in a large pot, add the corn, and simmer for 10–12 minutes, then add the roasted chipotle chile, mushrooms, garlic, cumin, cilantro, and tomatoes. Simmer for 5 min-utes to let the flavors infuse. Carefully drop the meatballs into the broth and cook gently for 8–10 minutes. Add the thinly sliced red chile and season with salt and freshly ground black pepper.

Put the meatballs into deep serving bowls and ladle the smoky-flavored broth over them. Serve the tortilla strips and guacamole separately so your guests can help themselves.

1 ear of corn

2 1/4 cups well-flavored chicken stock (preferably home-made)

1 chipotle chile, roasted (see p8)

1 1/2 cups white mushrooms, sliced

1/2 garlic clove, crushed

1/2 teaspoon ground cumin

A handful of fresh cilantro, stalks removed

2 plum tomatoes, skinned, seeded and cut into 1/4 inch dice

1 red jalapeño chile, thinly sliced into rings

Salt and freshly ground black pepper

For the albóndigas (meatballs):

1/2 onion, grated

1/2 pound ground pork

1 garlic clove, crushed

1 teaspoon cumin seeds

1/2 teaspoon dried red chili flakes

1 egg, beaten

5 tablespoons fresh white breadcrumbs

1 tablespoon chopped cilantro

For serving:

Fried tortilla strips

1/4 cup Guacamole en Molcajete (see p.153)

Chickpea and lentil mulligatawny
with smoked chicken and cumin yoghurt

Mulligatawny is one of those curious Anglo-Indian dishes that arose from the British occupation of India. The Victorians made it with onions, chicken, curry powder, dried coconut, and apple for sweetness. My version is much livelier, with chile, turmeric, and a smoked chicken and cumin garnish.

Melt the butter in a pot, add the onion, garlic, chili flakes and turmeric, and cook over low heat until softened. Add the soaked chickpeas and curry paste and cook for 5 minutes, then sprinkle in the gram flour and stir it in. Pour in the stock and bring to a boil, then simmer for 2 hours topping up with more liquid if it begins to get too dry. Stir in the lentils and simmer for 30–40 minutes, then add the mango chutney and apple, and cook for another 20 minutes.

For the cumin yoghurt, toast the cumin seeds in a frying pan over low heat until they are slightly darker and release their fragrance. Transfer to a spice mill or mortar and pestle, and grind to a powder. Stir the cumin into the yoghurt and set aside.

Pour the soup into a blender and blitz to a smooth purée. Return to a clean pot, add the coconut milk, and bring to a boil. Season to taste and serve, topped with the shredded smoked chicken and a little cumin yoghurt.

2 tablespoons sweet butter

1 onion, finely chopped

1 garlic clove, crushed

1 teaspoon dried red chili flakes

1/4 teaspoon ground turmeric

3/4 cup chickpeas, soaked in water overnight and then drained

2 tablespoons My Curry Paste (see p.154)

1 tablespoon gram (chickpea) flour

1 quart chicken or vegetable stock

1/2 cup Puy lentils

1 tablespoon mango chutney

1 Granny Smith apple, peeled, cored, and chopped

14 oz. can of coconut milk

2 cooked smoked chicken breasts, skin removed, and meat shredded

Salt and freshly ground black pepper

For the cumin yoghurt:

1/2 teaspoon cumin seeds

6 tablespoons Greek yoghurt or thick whole milk yoghurt

Spicy channa
(roasted chickpeas)

A wonderful and simple snack of spice-roasted chickpeas. It is normally sold by street vendors in India but it is easy to prepare at home and makes a great accompaniment to drinks.

Preheat the oven to 350°F. Toss the chickpeas with all the remaining ingredients, spread out on a baking sheet, and place in the oven to toast for about 8–10 minutes, until golden brown and crunchy. Store in an airtight container if not used immediately.

13/4 cups cooked chickpeas, well drained and dried

1/2 teaspoon cayenne pepper

2 tablespoons sweet butter, melted

1/2 teaspoon My Curry Paste (see p.154)

A pinch of brown sugar

Salt

Minced rabbit satay
with peanut and ginger dip

Marinating meat or fish and then grilling it on a skewer has been common for centuries, and is still popular today for barbecues. This Southeast Asian classic takes on a new twist when made with ground rabbit, but you could use chicken or pork instead. A fresh cucumber salad makes a good accompaniment.

For the satay, put all the ingredients except the rabbit and lemongrass in a blender or food processor, and blitz to a wet paste. Place the ground rabbit in a bowl, pour in the paste, and mix well with a wooden spoon. Cover and chill for 2 hours.
Meanwhile, make the dip: place all the ingredients in a pan and bring to a boil, then reduce the heat and simmer for 2–3 minutes. Pour into a bowl and let cool.
Remove the rabbit mixture from the refrigerator.

Dip your hands in a little hot water and then mold a heaped tablespoonful of the mixture around each prepared lemongrass skewer, making sure it encompasses it completely. Place the skewers under a hot broiler or, better still, over a hot barbecue and grill until golden, turning occasionally. They should take about 5–6 minutes to cook.
Serve the charred satay skewers with the peanut and ginger dip, or with Chili and Raisin Jam (see page 148) – or even with both.

1/2 teaspoon cumin seeds

1/2 teaspoon ground turmeric

1 garlic clove, chopped

3/4 inch piece of fresh ginger root, chopped

1 large shallot, chopped

11/2 teaspoons raw sugar

5 tablespoons peanut or vegetable oil

1 tablespoon sesame oil

2 teaspoons nam pla (Thai fish sauce)

1 lb. ground rabbit (taken from the saddle or hind legs)

8 lemongrass stalks, outer layers removed, cut into 6 inch lengths

Salt and freshly ground black pepper

For the peanut and ginger dip:

11/4 cups well-flavored chicken stock

2 teaspoons My Curry Paste (see p.154)

1 garlic clove, crushed

1 jalapeño chile, seeded and finely chopped

1/2 teaspoon honey

1/2 inch piece of fresh ginger root, finely chopped

6 tablespoons smooth peanut butter

1/2 teaspoon light soy sauce

A dash of wine vinegar

Crispy fried quail
with cashew and mint mole

This is a bit of a fusion dish, combining Oriental and Mexican techniques. The quail is prepared in a similar way to Peking duck – brushed with a rich glaze and then dried – but they are served with a spicy, minty Mexican mole. *Mole* means sauce or concoction. It is usually made with chiles and the color varies depending on what chiles are used.

Heat the maple syrup, chile, and lemon juice, and brush all over the quail. Place in a dry, well-ventilated area for 8–12 hours, then brush with the glaze again.

For the mole, pour boiling water over the ancho chiles and let soak for 1 hour, then drain. Place the chiles, onion, garlic, red peppers, tomatoes, and bread in a food processor and blitz to a paste, then add the cashews, spices, and mint, and blend again.

Heat the oil in a frying pan, then pour in the mole mixture and fry for 8–10 minutes. Add a little water to bring it to the consistency of a puréed soup, then season with the sugar and some salt and pepper. Keep warm.

Heat some vegetable oil in a deep-fat fryer or a large, deep pot to 325°F. Deep-fry the quails for 8–10 minutes, until tender and crisp, then drain on paper towels.

Pour the sauce on to serving plates and top with the fried quail. I like to serve this with black beans and guacamole.

1/4 cup maple syrup

1 New Mexican dried red chile or
 1/2 teaspoon chili powder

Juice of 1 lemon

8 quails, boned and cut in half

Vegetable oil for deep-frying

For the cashew and mint mole:

2 dried ancho chiles, roasted (see p.8)

1 onion, roughly chopped

2 garlic cloves, crushed

1 red pepper, trimmed and seeded

7 ounce can of plum tomatoes

3 slices of white bread, crusts removed

3/4 cup cashews

1/2 teaspoon ground cinnamon

1/2 teaspoon ground allspice

1 bunch of mint (about 2 ounces)

1/4 cup vegetable oil

A pinch of sugar

Salt and freshly ground black pepper

Potato and shrimp bhajias
on saffron, cucumber and tomato raita

Make the raita by mixing all the ingredients together, then set aside.

Shred the potatoes – preferably on a mandoline, although you could do them on the coarse side of a grater. In a bowl, mix together all the dry ingredients for the batter, add the curry paste, and then gradually add the water, stirring until combined. Season with salt. Add the potatoes, chiles, and cilantro, and toss well together.

Heat some vegetable oil in a deep-fat fryer or a large, deep pot to 350°F. Season the shrimp with salt and ground black pepper. Using a large table-spoon, scoop a mound of the batter mixture into the palm of your hand, then press a shrimp into the center and re-shape into a ball, so the shrimp is in the middle. Repeat to make 16 bhajias. Fry them in batches in the hot oil for 3–4 minutes, until crisp and cooked through, then drain on paper towels.

Place the bhajias on a bed of the raita, on individual serving plates, garnish with fresh cilantro, and serve immediately.

3/4 lb. potatoes, peeled
   (about 3 medium potatoes)
2 green Thai chiles, seeded and
   chopped
2 ounces fresh cilantro (about 1 small
   bunch), chopped, plus some cilantro
   leaves to garnish
Vegetable oil for deep-frying
16 raw tiger shrimp, peeled and
   de-veined
Salt and freshly ground black pepper

For the raita:
1/2 cucumber, peeled, seeded, and cut
   into 1/2 inch dice
6 tablespoons Greek yoghurt or a thick,
   whole milk yoghurt
1/4 teaspoon saffron strands, steeped in
   2 tablespoons boiling water
1 teaspoon ground cumin
1 teaspoon ground coriander
1 tablespoon chopped mint
4 plum tomatoes, skinned, seeded
   and cut into 1/2 inch dice

For the batter:
1 cup (chickpea) flour
1/3 cup ground rice
1/2 teaspoon baking powder
1/2 teaspoon chili powder
1/2 teaspoon ground turmeric
1/4 teaspoon asafetida
1 tablespoon My Curry Paste (see p.154)
1 cup water

Hot Chinese mustard chicken wings

Using a sharp knife, cut off the tip of each chicken wing. At this stage you can either leave the wings as they are or cut through the joint to make two smaller pieces.

In a large bowl, combine all the remaining ingredients, then add the chicken wings and mix thoroughly so they are well coated. Cover and let marinate for up to 12 hours.

Preheat the oven to 400°F. Remove the chicken wings from their marinade and place in a baking dish or pan, then roast in the oven for about 30 minutes. Pour the marinade into a small pan and bring to a boil. Simmer until reduced and thickened enough to coat the back of a spoon. Use this reduced marinade to baste the wings as they cook; it will form a wonderful glaze. I like to serve the chicken wings hot but they are equally delicious cold.

20 chicken wings
2/3 cup hoisin sauce
Juice of 1 lime
1/4 cup nam pla (Thai fish sauce)
2 garlic cloves, crushed
1 tablespoon honey
1 tablespoon hot Chinese mustard
2 tablespoons chopped cilantro
2 tablespoons mirin (Japanese sweet rice wine)

Roasted skate escabeche
with tarragon mustard dressing

Escabeche is a Spanish dish of cooked fish lightly pickled in a piquant marinade. This version uses skate wings, and the marinade is livened up with tarragon mustard, roasted red and yellow peppers, citrus juice, cilantro and capers, for a vibrant mix of colors and flavors.

Preheat the oven to 375°F. Place the skate wings on a baking tray, brush with half the oil, and season with salt and pepper. Roast for 10–12 minutes or until just cooked. Remove from the oven and let cool.

Heat the remaining oil in a pan, add the onion, and cook over low heat for 3–4 minutes, until just softened. Add the coriander seeds, chile, and garlic, and cook for a further minute.

In a bowl, combine the citrus juices and zest with all the remaining ingredients to make a marinade. Add the softened onion and chile mixture, then season to taste.

With a sharp knife, carefully remove all the bones from the skate. Add the meat to the marinade, cover, and leave in the fridge overnight.

Arrange the fish and marinaded ingredients stacked in a pile, on a large serving platter or individual plates. Drizzle the marinade juices over them, and serve with lots of crusty bread.

4 x 12 ounce prepared skate wings
1/2 cup virgin olive oil
1 red onion, thinly sliced
1 teaspoon coriander seeds
1 serrano chile, thinly sliced
1 garlic clove, crushed
Juice and zest of 1 orange
Juice and zest of 1 lime
Juice and zest of 1 lemon
1 red and 1 yellow pepper, roasted, peeled and cut into strips
A handful of cilantro leaves
1 tablespoon cocktail capers, rinsed and drained
1 teaspoon tarragon mustard
1/2 cup dry white wine
1/3 cup tarragon vinegar
1 tablespoon brown sugar
Salt and freshly ground black pepper

SALMON RILLETTES

Crispy corn tortillas
with chile con queso and merguez

Heat some vegetable oil in a deep-fat fryer or a large, deep pot to 375°F and fry the tortilla quarters until crisp and golden. Remove with a slotted spoon and drain on paper towels. Keep warm while you prepare the sauce.

Put 2 tablespoons of the frying oil in another pan, add the onion, garlic, tomato, chiles, and merguez, and cook gently for 5–6 minutes, until the onion is tender. Add the white wine and increase the heat to evaporate it. Reduce the heat again to low, add the cheese, and stir until completely melted.

Arrange the tortilla wedges on a flat serving plate and pour the spicy cheese sauce over them. Serve immediately.

Vegetable oil for deep-frying

8 x 6 inch corn tortillas, cut into quarters

1 small red onion, finely chopped

2 garlic cloves, crushed

1 tomato, cut into large pieces

4 green jalapeño chiles, seeded and thinly sliced

1/4 lb. merguez sausage, cut into small dice

1/2 cup dry white wine

11/2 cups grated Cheddar cheese

Salmon rillettes
with Asian spices, and apple and beet relish

Season the salmon with salt and pepper, then steam it until just cooked. Let cool completely.

Place the salmon in a bowl and, using a fork, flake the fish into small pieces. Add the curry paste, cilantro, ginger, and shallots. Bind with the mayonnaise, just to bring it together, then check the seasoning and adjust if necessary.

Place a 21/2–3inch ring mold or pastry cutter in the center of a serving plate. Fill the mold with the salmon mixture, level it off with a knife, then carefully remove the mold. Repeat on 3 more serving plates.

For the relish, place the beet, apples, ginger, and basil in a bowl. In another bowl mix together the lime juice, mustard, and oil to form an emulsion, then pour this over the beet and apple, and mix together gently. Season to taste. Serve with the salmon rillettes.

11/2 lbs. fresh salmon fillet, skinned

2 teaspoons My Curry Paste (see p.154)

2 tablespoons chopped cilantro

1 inch fresh ginger root, finely chopped

2 shallots (or scallions), finely chopped

1/4 cup well-flavored mayonnaise

Salt and freshly ground black pepper

For the apple and beet relish:

1 cooked beet, shredded

2 Granny Smith apples, peeled, cored, and shredded

1 inch piece of fresh ginger root, finely shredded

5 basil leaves, shredded

Juice of 1 lime

1/2 teaspoon Dijon mustard

6 tablespoons olive oil

Three-pepper salmon
with grappa, dill, and lemon crème fraîche

Mix together the lemon juice and zest, crème fraîche, and black pepper. With a sharp carving knife, thinly slice the salmon on the diagonal. Cut a rectangular sheet of wax paper approximately 16 x 8 inches and brush it liberally with the olive oil. Arrange the salmon slices on the paper, overlapping each slice as you go. Season with salt, then brush on the grappa, sprinkle over them the green and pink peppercorns, and then scatter over that the chopped dill. Top with the crème fraîche, carefully smearing it over the surface with the aid of a palette knife dipped in hot water.

Starting at a long side of the rectangle, carefully roll up the salmon as if making a jelly roll, holding on to the paper, which will be released when the salmon is rolled. Chill for 1 hour.

To serve, cut the roll into 8 slices and place on serving plates. Toss the salad greens and herbs with the vinaigrette, and use to garnish the salmon. Serve with the lemon wedges

HOT TIP To make cracked black pepper, put the peppercorns in a small bowl and break them up roughly with the end of a rolling pin, or use a mortar and pestle.

Juice and zest of 1 lemon

3 tablespoons crème fraîche (if unavailable, use heavy cream)

1/2 teaspoon black peppercorns, cracked (see Hot Tip)

11/2 lbs. very fresh salmon fillet, skinned

3 tablespoons olive oil

2 tablespoons grappa

1 teaspoon green peppercorns, lightly crushed with a fork

1 teaspoon pink peppercorns, lightly crushed with a fork

6 tablespoons roughly chopped dill

1 lemon, cut into wedges, for garnishing

Salt

For the herb salad:

2 ounces frisée lettuce (a good handful)

2 ounces young spinach leaves (a large handful)

2 tablespoons each of dill, chervil, chives, and basil

2 tablespoons plain vinaigrette of your choice

Balsamic sardines
on crushed mustard potatoes

Heat a non-stick frying pan, then add 2 table-spoons of the oil and fry the sardine fillets for 1 minute on each side, until well seasoned but not colored. Place the sardine fillets in a large earthen-ware dish. Add all the remaining ingredients to the pan, bring to a boil, and simmer for 10 minutes, then pour this mixture over the fillets. Let stand for at least 3 hours, turning the fish at least twice during this time.

Meanwhile, cook the potatoes in a pot of boiling salted water until just tender, then drain and leave until cool enough to handle. Peel the potatoes and place them in a bowl. Crush with a fork until they are chunky, then stir in the olive oil, chile, and Dijon mustard. Finally add the chopped cilantro.

To serve, put the warm crushed potatoes on individual serving plates and top with the marinated sardine fillets. Drizzle a little marinade on top.

1 cup olive oil

8 small sardines, filleted

5 tablespoons white wine vinegar

2 tablespoons balsamic vinegar

1 tablespoon sugar

1 small onion, thinly sliced

1 teaspoon black peppercorns

1 teaspoon coriander seeds

1 small dried red chile

1 fresh bay leaf

1 garlic clove, crushed

For the mustard potatoes:

10 ounces new potatoes

1/2 cup olive oil

1 red chile, seeded and finely chopped

1 teaspoon Dijon mustard

1 tablespoon chopped cilantro

Barbecue-spiced squid
with cayenne–blue cheese aïoli

This idea came from a trip to Houston, where I did a promotion at a hotel. The chef took me to a restaurant called Pignetti's, where we drank tequilas all night and the owner brought us a dish of spicy deep-fried squid with a blue cheese sauce. Here is my slightly adapted version – tequilas optional.

First make the aïoli: mix the egg yolks together, in a bowl with the garlic, lemon juice, and a little salt. Add the oil, drop by drop at first, whisking constantly until the mixture is smooth and thick. Gently mix the blue cheese with 3 tablespoons of hot water to form a paste, then mix into the sauce. Finally add the cayenne pepper and some more salt if needed.

Slice the squid bodies into rings 1/4 inch thick; leave the tentacles in large pieces. Mix together the spice mix, cornstarch, and baking powder. Heat some vegetable oil in a deep-fat fryer or a large, deep pot to 375°F. Dip the squid pieces in the milk and then in the spice mix, shaking off any excess. Fry in batches in the hot oil for about 1–2 minutes, until brown and crisp; do not overcook or the squid will be tough. Remove the squid and drain on paper towels, then sprinkle with salt and Szechuan pepper. Serve immediately, with the aïoli and lemon wedges.

1¼ lbs. cleaned small or
  medium squid
2 tablespoons Barbecue spice mix
  (see p.157)
1 cup cornstarch
1 teaspoon baking powder
Vegetable oil for deep-frying
2/3 cup whole milk
1 lemon, cut into wedges
Salt and ground Szechuan pepper
For the cayenne–blue cheese aïoli:
2 egg yolks
1 garlic clove, crushed
Juice of 1/2 lemon
3/4 cup virgin olive oil
3 ounces blue cheese (3/4 cup)
1/4 teaspoon cayenne pepper

HOT TIP The safest way to deep-fry is in a thermostatically controlled deep-fat fryer but you can also use a large, deep pot. Never fill it more than a third full with oil and, to avoid the danger of flare-ups, make sure the pan covers the heat source completely. The oil should be hot enough to form bubbles around the food as soon as you put it in. Don't overcrowd the pot, as this will cause the temperature to drop, and remember to dry the food first if necessary, to prevent the oil splattering.

Chargrilled squid fajitas
with scallions, pepper, and arugula

This makes a great snack and is very quick to prepare. Fajitas are soft filled tortillas, usually prepared with meat such as chicken or beef. Squid makes a good light alternative. Serve with your favorite salsa, guacamole, and sour cream.

Cook the peppers and scallions on a ridged grill pan until charred and tender, then remove from the pan and keep warm. Place the squid, including the tentacles, on the grill pan (it should be very hot), season with salt and pepper, and grill for 1–2 minutes, turning once.

Shred the squid, peppers, and scallions, and place in a bowl. Add the garlic, chile sauce, lime juice, cumin, and arugula, and season to taste. Quickly heat the tortillas on the grill for 10 seconds on each side, until slightly charred. Arrange the squid and vegetables in the warm tortillas, fold one end of the tortilla over the filling and roll up. Serve immediately.

1 red pepper, cut in half and seeded

1 green pepper, cut in half and seeded

8 scallions

4 medium-sized squid, cleaned

1 garlic clove, crushed

6 tablespoons chile sauce

Juice of 1/2 small lime

1 teaspoon ground cumin

A handful of wild arugula leaves

8 x 6–7 inch flour tortillas

Salt and freshly ground black pepper

Roasted mussels
with Indian green chutney

This unusual method of cooking mussels seals in all their natural juices and flavors. It's great served with Grilled black pepper nans (see page 140).

In a blender, blitz together the cilantro leaves, ginger, garlic, chiles, cardamom, lemon juice, and water to make a smooth paste. Pour into a small bowl and set aside.

In a small frying pan, heat 2 tablespoons of the oil until hot but not smoking. Add the cumin seeds and mustard seeds. When they begin to pop, stir in the turmeric, some salt, and the cilantro purée. Add another 3 tablespoons of the oil and cook for 1 minute, then remove from the heat.

Preheat the oven to 400°F. Scrub the mussels thoroughly under cold running water, pulling out the beards and discarding any open mussels that do not close when tapped on the work surface. Place the mussels in a baking pan, pour the remaining oil over them, and mix together. Scatter the cilantro stalks on top, and place in the oven for 3–4 minutes or until the shells have opened. Remove from the oven and discard the cilantro stalks.

Arrange the mussels in a large serving bowl, pour the chutney over them, and serve immediately.

HOT TIP This versatile chutney can also be stirred into soups or served with vegetables.

2 ounces cilantro leaves (a small bunch) (set aside the stalks)

1 inch piece of fresh ginger root, chopped

2 garlic cloves, chopped

2 green jalapeño chiles, seeded and chopped

1/2 teaspoon ground cardamom

Juice of 1 lemon

1/4 cup water

2/3 cup olive oil

1/2 teaspoon cumin seeds

1/2 teaspoon brown mustard seeds

1/2 teaspoon ground turmeric

11/2 lbs. mussels

Salt and freshly ground black pepper

✱ Chilled mussels
in harissa salsa

I have very fond memories of my late father, who had an infinite love of seafood, especially mussels. He would eat them at any opportunity, at any time of day, and he taught me to appreciate their delicate qualities, too. Here is one of my favorite ways of serving them, bathed in a spicy vinaigrette. I know he would have loved this recipe.

Scrub the mussels thoroughly under cold running water, pulling out the beards and discarding any open mussels that do not close when tapped on the work surface. Place the mussels in a large pot, scatter in the onion, garlic, cilantro stalks, and chili flakes, then pour in the wine and enough water just to cover. Put a lid on the pot and place over high heat to steam for about 5 minutes, or until the mussels have opened, shaking the pot halfway through to redistribute the mussels. Drain in a colander, reserving the cooking liquor, and set aside. Strain the liquor through a fine mesh strainer.

For the salsa, mix together all the ingredients in a bowl.

Remove the mussels from their shells but retain half of each shell. Add the warm mussels to the salsa with 1/4 cup of the strained mussel stock. Let cool, then chill for 1 hour.

To serve, place a mussel on each half shell and arrange on a serving dish. Spoon the salsa over them and serve at room temperature.

HOT TIP Like all shellfish, mussels must be bought alive. Look for ones that are tightly shut, heavy for their size, and smell good. Always discard any with open or broken shells and, if in doubt about their freshness, throw them away. Wrapped in wet newspaper, mussels will keep for up to 2 days in the fridge.

11/2 lbs. very fresh mussels

1 onion, chopped

1 garlic clove, finely sliced

A few cilantro stalks

A good pinch of dried red chili flakes

1 cup dry white wine

For the harissa salsa:

2 plum tomatoes, skinned, seeded, and finely chopped

1 small onion, finely chopped

1 garlic clove, crushed

2 tablespoons chopped cilantro

3 tablespoons white wine vinegar

1 tablespoon maple syrup

1/2 teaspoon Harissa (see p.156)

Juice of 1/2 lemon

1 red, 1 green, and 1 yellow pepper, roasted, peeled, and finely diced

Curried crab tart
with smoky guacamole and mango dressing

Preheat the oven to 400°F. In a bowl, combine the crabmeat, mayonnaise, curry paste, cream, and chile. Season to taste, then chill while you prepare the pastry dough.

Roll out the dough until it is 1/4 inch thick and then use to line four 31/2 inch removable-bottomed fluted tart pans. Line them with wax paper and fill with baking beans, then bake blind for 5–6 minutes. Remove the beans and paper from the pastry shells and bake for a further 2–3 minutes. Remove from the oven and let cool. Reduce the oven temperature to 350°F.

Mix together all the ingredients for the mango dressing, season to taste, and leave for 15–20 minutes for the flavors to blend.

Put a heaped tablespoon of the guacamole in each of the pastry shells, then top with the crabmeat mixture. Return to the oven to glaze for about 5–6 minutes. Turn the tarts out on to serving plates, place a little of the mango dressing around each one, and serve. A little fresh salad goes well with this dish.

10 ounces fresh crabmeat

1/4 cup well-flavored mayonnaise

2 teaspoons Red Thai Curry Paste
 (see p.155)

1 tablespoon heavy cream

1 jalapeño chile, seeded and chopped

pastry dough, enough for 1 pie

1/4 cup Smoky Guacamole en
 Molcajete (see p.153)

Salt and freshly ground black pepper

For the mango dressing:

1/2 mango, peeled and cut into
 1/4 inch dice

2 plum tomatoes, skinned, seeded
 and cut into 1/4 inch dice

1 shallot, chopped

Juice of 2 limes

1 tablespoon chopped cilantro

1 small serrano chile, seeded and
 chopped

1/4 cup vegetable oil

Blackened oysters
on spring greens with tomato and horseradish salsa

For the salsa, mix all the ingredients together in a bowl and let marinate for up to 1 hour, to allow the flavors to develop.

Shuck the oysters (see Hot Tip below), then wash the shells and set aside.

Remove the stalks from the spring greens, cut the greens into small pieces, and wash well. Cook in boiling salted water for 5–6 minutes, then drain thoroughly. Heat 1 tablespoon of the olive oil in a frying pan, add the bacon, and fry until crisp. Then add the spring greens and sauté for 2–3 minutes,

until tender. Season and keep warm.

Warm the washed oyster shells in a low oven for 5 minutes. Dry the shucked oysters and dredge them with the spice mix. Heat the remaining olive oil in a large frying pan and fry the oysters over high heat for 30–40 seconds, until they are just cooked and have formed a spicy crust.

Divide the greens and bacon between the heated oyster shells, then put a spicy oyster in each shell and coat with a little salsa. Garnish with the lemon wedges. Serve the remaining salsa separately.

20 large rock oysters
3/4 lb. spring greens
1/4 cup olive oil
4 ounces back bacon or Canadian
  bacon, chopped
2 tablespoons Blackened Cajun spice mix
  (see p.157)
1 lemon, cut into wedges, for garnishing
Salt and freshly ground black pepper
For the tomato and horseradish salsa:
1/2 lb. plum tomatoes, finely diced
1/2 red onion, finely chopped
Juice of 1 lime
2 tablespoons maple syrup
1 red chile, seeded and chopped
1 tablespoon cilantro leaves
1 teaspoon grated horseradish root

HOT TIP To open oysters you need an oyster knife or a short, strong-bladed knife. Wrap your hand in a tea towel to protect it, then take hold of an oyster and insert the knife blade between the shells, next to the hinge. Twist the knife to lever open the top shell, then cut the muscle connecting the oyster to the shell. Next, loosen the muscle connecting the oyster to the bottom shell and take out the oyster.

Grilled scallops
with black bean and citrus chili oil vinaigrette

Mix together all the ingredients for the vinaigrette, then place the scallops in it. Cover with plastic wrap and leave in the fridge for 4 hours to marinate.

When ready to serve, heat a ridged grill pan and brush it with a little oil. Remove the scallops from

the vinaigrette and place on the grill to cook for 30 seconds on each side. Arrange on serving plates.

Remove the cilantro sprigs from the vinaigrette and, using a slotted spoon, spoon the vinaigrette ingredients over the scallops. Drizzle over them a little of the liquid, and garnish with fresh cilantro leaves. Serve immediately.

8 medium-large scallops, cleaned
A little oil for grilling
Cilantro leaves, for garnishing
For the vinaigrette:
Juice and zest of 2 oranges
Juice and zest of 4 limes
1 teaspoon finely chopped fresh ginger
2 garlic cloves, thinly sliced
4 scallions, shredded
1/2 cup cooked black beans
2 plum tomatoes, skinned, seeded
  and diced
1/4 cup Chili oil (see p.152)
1 green jalapeño chile, thinly sliced
1/4 teaspoon smoked paprika
4 sprigs of cilantro

Deviled scallops
in bacon with garlic–pea purée and sage butter

Deviling is a good old-fashioned British technique, using Worcestershire sauce, mustard, or cayenne to spice up foods such as chicken, crab, and bloaters, the famous preserved herring from Great Yarmouth, England. Here, scallops are given a generous dusting of cayenne pepper to make a favorite dish of mine.

Preheat the oven to 400°F. Place the unpeeled garlic cloves on a baking sheet, pour the oil over them, and roast for 15–20 minutes, until lightly charred and very soft. Remove from the oven and let cool. Squeeze the garlic flesh out of its skin and place in a blender.

Cook the peas in boiling salted water until very tender, then drain well and add to the blender, along with 2 tablespoons of the butter. Season with salt and pepper and blitz until smooth and silky in texture. Keep warm.

Dust the scallops well with the cayenne pepper and a little salt, then wrap in the bacon and secure with a toothpick. Place under a hot broiler or on a ridged grill pan for 2–3 minutes on each side, until the bacon is crisp and the scallops just cooked.

To serve, place a little mound of pea purée on each serving plate and top with a scallop. Keep warm. Heat a small frying pan until very hot, then add the remaining butter and cook until foaming and nutty in fragrance.

Add the sage leaves and lemon juice, then pour the foaming butter over and around the scallops, and serve immediately.

5 garlic cloves

3 tablespoons olive oil

11/2 cups frozen peas

11/4 sticks (about 2/3 cup) sweet butter

*4 very large sea scallops
(or 8 medium-sized ones), cleaned,
coral removed*

1 teaspoon cayenne pepper

*8 slices of back bacon or Canadian
bacon*

10 small sage leaves

Juice of 1/2 lemon

Salt and freshly ground black pepper

Black sesame lobster tempura
with Japanese slaw and wasabi vinaigrette

This intriguing dish may sound complicated but in fact there's very little cooking involved. The Japanese slaw is cool and refreshing, and adds a wonderful crunch to the deep-fried lobster.

Cut each lobster tail in half down the center but leave the claws whole.

In a bowl, whisk together the eggs and water until pale and foamy. Add the baking soda and flour, and mix lightly to make a batter. It should remain a little lumpy.

For the vinaigrette, place the ginger and wasabi paste in a bowl, then whisk in the rice vinegar, mirin, and soy sauce. Whisk in the oil a little at a time to form an emulsion. Stir in the hot water. Add all the ingredients for the slaw and mix well together. Leave for 10–15 minutes to let the flavors meld.

Heat some vegetable oil in a deep-fat fryer or a large, deep pot to 350°F. Dip the lobster tails and claws in the tempura batter, sprinkle liberally with the sesame seeds, and fry for 2–3 minutes or until crisp. Remove and drain on paper towels. Put the lobster on 4 serving plates, one half tail and one claw per person, garnish with a heap of coleslaw, and drizzle over them any remaining dressing, then serve immediately.

2 x 1½ lb. lobsters, cooked,
  shell removed
2 eggs
½ cup iced water
A good pinch of baking soda
⅔ cup all purpose flour
Vegetable oil for deep-frying
1½ teaspoons black sesame seeds
For the wasabi vinaigrette:
2 inch piece of fresh ginger root,
  finely grated
½ teaspoon wasabi paste
2 tablespoons rice vinegar
2 tablespoons mirin (Japanese sweet
  rice wine)
1 teaspoon light soy sauce
½ cup vegetable oil
2 tablespoons hot water
For the slaw:
1 carrot, finely shredded
2 ounces red cabbage,
  finely shredded (about 1 cup)
3 ounces celeriac, finely shredded
  (about ⅔ cup)
2 ounces beansprouts
2 ounces arame or hijiki seaweed

HOT TIP The wasabi vinaigrette can also be served with carpaccio of beef or as a dressing for a meat salad.

Marinated goat cheese
with nectarine and honey peppercorn dressing

Mix together all the marinade ingredients in a small dish, then add the goat cheese. Cover and refrigerate for at least 4 hours or, better still, overnight. Transfer the cheeses to a small baking dish and strain the oil through a fine mesh strainer; you will need 5 tablespoons of it for the dressing.

For the dressing, crush the pink peppercorns in a bowl, then add the mustard and honey and blend together. Whisk in a tablespoon of the reserved marinade to form an emulsion, then whisk in the vinegar, followed by 1/4 cup of the marinade. Add the hot water and adjust the seasoning.

Warm the goat cheese under a hot broiler or in a moderate oven for 2–3 minutes, until just heated through, but do not let it melt. To serve, place the spinach leaves in a bowl with the walnuts and nectarine slices, drizzle over them the pink peppercorn dressing, and season lightly. Put the cheeses on individual serving plates and sprinkle with some lightly crushed pink peppercorns, then garnish with a mound of salad, and serve. Good crusty bread makes an ideal accompaniment to this dish.

4 crottins de Chavignol (or use a
 12 ounce goat cheese log, sliced into
 quarters)
1 bag of young spinach leaves
2 tablespoons walnut halves
1 ripe but firm nectarine, pitted and
 thinly sliced
Salt and freshly ground black pepper

For the marinade:

2/3 cup olive oil
2 garlic cloves, crushed
1 bay leaf
1/2 teaspoon thyme leaves
1/2 teaspoon rosemary

For the dressing:

1 teaspoon pink peppercorns, plus
 extra for garnishing
1/2 teaspoon Dijon mustard
1 teaspoon honey
1 tablespoon white wine vinegar
1 tablespoon hot water

HOT TIP If you are weight conscious, replace half the oil in the dressing with reduced chicken stock.

fish and seafood

Roast cod on smoked salmon
and cabbage hash with horseradish butter

Bring a large pot of water to a boil, add a little salt, then add the shredded cabbage and return to a boil. Reduce the heat to a simmer and cook for 5–8 minutes. Drain off most of the water, leaving only a little in the pan. Add the caraway seeds and cream, and cook over a gentle heat for about 5 minutes, until the cabbage is well cooked and just bound by the cream. Adjust the seasoning and stir in the smoked salmon. Keep warm.

Heat a large frying pan, add the oil and 2 table-spoons of the butter, then fry the cod, skin-side first, for 3–4 minutes per side, until golden and crisp. When it is done, divide the cabbage between 4 serving plates, top with a crisp piece of cod, and sprinkle a little sea salt over it.

Heat a small frying pan, melt the remaining butter in it, then add the lemon juice and finally the horseradish. Pour the sauce over the cod and cabbage hash and serve immediately, with plain mashed potatoes.

1/2 white or pale green cabbage, finely shredded

1 teaspoon caraway seeds

2 tablespoons heavy cream

3 ounces smoked salmon, shredded

1/4 cup olive oil

1 stick (1/2 cup) sweet butter

7 ounce cod fillets (skin on)

Juice of 1/2 lemon

11/2 teaspoons finely grated horse-radish root

Sea salt and freshly ground black pepper

Pepper-grilled swordfish
with preserved lemon oil and wilted chard

Swordfish is fairly robust, so occasionally I like to treat it in the same way as meat – here it is coated with black pepper, like a steak. Swiss chard makes the ideal accompaniment but if you can't get hold of any, you could always use spinach instead.

Heat half the oil in a small pan, add the garlic and tomatoes, and cook over low heat for 2 minutes. Stir in the dried chili, preserved lemons, and lemon juice and zest, then remove from the heat and let infuse.

Heat another 3 tablespoons of the oil in a pan, add the chard and cook over low heat for 10–15 minutes, until wilted. Season to taste and keep warm while you cook the fish.

Heat a broiler to its highest setting. Coat the swordfish steaks with the remaining oil, then coat both sides of the fish with the cracked peppercorns and season with a little salt. Broil for 2–3 minutes on each side. Place each steak on a bed of the Swiss chard, coat with the lemon and tomato dressing, and serve immediately.

2/3 cup olive oil
1 garlic clove, crushed
4 plum tomatoes, skinned, seeded and cut into small dice
1/2 teaspoon dried red chili flakes
1 tablespoon finely chopped salted preserved lemons (see Hot Tip)
Juice and zest of 1 lemon
12 ounces Swiss chard, coarsely shredded
6 ounce swordfish steaks
1 teaspoon coarsely cracked black peppercorns (see Hot Tip on p.28)
Salt and freshly ground black pepper

HOT TIP Preserved lemons are a staple of Moroccan cuisine, typically used in tagines or in fish dishes such as this one. When a recipe calls for preserved lemon, use the rind only, as the flesh tastes too briny.

Smoked mackerel fishcakes
with horseradish mayo

For the horseradish mayo, mix all the ingredients together and season to taste.

Mix the smoked mackerel with the mashed potatoes, egg yolks, dill, and anchovy paste, and season to taste. Chill the mixture until firm enough to handle, then, on a floured surface, shape it into flat cakes, using floured hands and a metal spatula.

In a shallow bowl, lightly whisk the egg whites to break them up. Spread the flour out on one large plate, and the breadcrumbs on another. Dip the fishcakes in the flour, then in the egg white, and finally in the breadcrumbs. Shallow-fry them in a little hot oil until golden brown, turning once.

Serve with the horseradish mayo.

1 lb. smoked mackerel, flaked
2 cups mashed potatoes
2 eggs, separated
1 tablespoon chopped dill
1 teaspoon anchovy paste
1/2 cup all purpose flour
2 cups fresh white breadcrumbs
Vegetable oil for shallow-frying
Salt and freshly ground black pepper
For the horseradish mayo:
1/2 cup good-quality mayonnaise
1 tablespoon grated horseradish root
1 tablespoon chopped dill
1 tablespoon grain mustard
A dash of wine vinegar
1 teaspoon lemon juice

* Jerk mackerel
with jollof rice and Caribbean mojo

The Caribbean term, jerk, originally referred to marinated meats that were covered with ashes and cooked slowly in a pit. Today it can mean a seasoning mixture, the style of cooking, or the finished dish. The spice rub in this recipe is based on traditional Jamaican jerk seasoning. It is great rubbed on just about any meat or fish before broiling. You can also buy jerk sauces or seasoning powders.

Jollof is a gently spiced tomato-flavored rice. I picked up the recipe for it when I was working in the Caribbean.

Make 3 deep slashes through the skin on each side of the mackerel pieces and season with salt. Put 2 tablespoons of the olive oil in a bowl, add the thyme, spices, sugar, scallions, and Worcestershire sauce, and mix well. Smear this mixture all over the mackerel and let marinate for 1 hour.

Meanwhile prepare the jollof rice: heat the butter in a large pot, add the onion, garlic, and allspice, and sweat over medium heat until softened. Add the rice and cook for 1 minute, until the butter is absorbed – do not brown. Stir in the tomato paste, then pour in the stock, season to taste, and bring to a boil. Reduce the heat and cook gently until all the liquid has been absorbed and the rice is tender.

Preheat the broiler to its highest setting. Clean the mackerel of any excess marinade, then place it on a broiler pan. Pour the remaining oil over it and broil about 6–8 inches from the heat for 10–12 minutes or until browned and cooked through. Serve on the jollof rice with the Caribbean mojo.

2 x 11/2 lb. cleaned mackerel, head and tail removed, fish cut in half crosswise
5 tablespoons olive oil
1 teaspoon dried thyme
1 teaspoon ground allspice
1/4 teaspoon grated nutmeg
1/4 teaspoon ground cinnamon
1 tablespoon freshly ground black pepper
1/2 teaspoon dried red chili flakes
1/2 teaspoon sugar
6 scallions, finely chopped
1 teaspoon Worcestershire sauce
1 quantity of Caribbean mojo (see p.151)
Salt and freshly ground black pepper

For the jollof rice:
1/2 stick (1/4 cup) sweet butter
1/2 onion, chopped
3 garlic cloves, crushed
1/2 teaspoon ground allspice
11/4 cups long grain rice
1 tablespoon tomato paste
2 cups chicken stock (or water)

Fried baby sole
with banana, flaked almonds, and deviled sauce

There is a classic dish called Sole Caprice, consisting of fried sole, mango chutney, banana, and sauce Robert, which I've always loved. Here's a lighter, fresher version that retains all the charm of the original.

For the sauce, melt 1/2 tablespoon of the butter in a pan, add the shallots and peppercorns, and sweat until softened. Add the thyme and bay leaf. Pour in the wine and vinegar and bring to a boil, then add the stock and simmer until the sauce has reduced by half its volume. Cut the remaining butter into cubes and whisk into the sauce a little at a time. Strain through a fine mesh strainer and season to taste with cayenne pepper and salt. Keep it warm while you prepare the fish.

Season the fish fillets liberally with salt and pepper. Mix the cilantro and panko crumbs together. Dip the fillets in the melted butter, then in the cilantro crumbs. Heat the oil in a large frying pan and then add 2 tablespoons of the melted butter. Carefully add the fish fillets and cook for 2–3 minutes on each side, until golden. Keep warm.

Heat the remaining butter in a separate frying pan, add the bananas and brown sugar, and cook until lightly caramelized. Season the sauce lightly with salt and pepper.

To serve, place a tablespoon of mango chutney on each serving plate and top with 4 fillets of sole. Then arrange the caramelized bananas and flaked almonds on top, and pour a little of the deviled sauce around the fish.

Skinned fillets from 4 x 12–14 ounce
  baby sole
2 tablespoons chopped cilantro
1 cup panko crumbs (see Hot Tip on
  p.47) or dried white breadcrumbs
1 stick (1/2 cup) sweet butter, melted
1/4 cup vegetable oil
3 bananas, peeled, and cut on the
  diagonal into slices 1/2 inch thick
1 teaspoon brown sugar
1/4 cup mango chutney
2 tablespoons slivered almonds, toasted
Salt and freshly ground black pepper
For the deviled sauce:
1/2 stick (1/4 cup) cold sweet butter
2 shallots, finely chopped
6 black peppercorns, crushed
1 sprig of thyme
1 small bay leaf
1/3 cup dry white wine
1/3 cup white wine vinegar
2/3 cup meat stock
A pinch of cayenne pepper

Sea bass
with deviled crab and red pepper chutney

Ideally, the chutney should be made at least 3 days in advance to give the flavors time to mellow.

For the chutney, sweat the onion and garlic in the oil for 4–5 minutes, until softened but not colored. Add the roasted peppers, ginger, and chile, and cook for 5 minutes, then stir in the vinegar and brown sugar and cook for another 5 minutes. Add the raisins and tomato sauce and simmer for 20 minutes, until the chutney is very reduced and syrupy. Remove from the heat and let cool.

Cut the bass fillets in half to obtain 4 nice bass supremes. Mix together the crabmeat, mayonnaise, chiles, ginger, mace, and cilantro, then stir in the breadcrumbs and season with salt and pepper. Spoon the mixture on top of each bass fillet in a layer about 1/4 inch thick. Place in the fridge until needed.

For the sauce, put the chicken stock, ginger, and lemongrass in a pan and simmer for 10–15 minutes, until reduced by one third in volume. Whisk in the olive oil, season to taste, and then strain through a fine mesh strainer. Keep warm.

Preheat the oven to 450°F. Heat 2 tablespoons of the olive oil in a large pot, add the spinach, and cook for 2–3 minutes, until wilted. Season and drain well.

Heat the remaining oil in a large ovenproof frying pan over high heat. Add the bass fillets and leave until sealed underneath, then transfer to the oven to cook through and crisp up the crab topping. To serve, divide the spinach between 4 shallow soup plates, top with the baked bass, garnish with a spoonful of chutney, then pour a little of the sauce lightly around the bass.

HOT TIP Panko crumbs are dried breadcrumbs used in oriental cooking, especially for deep-fried dishes. They can be hard to obtain but it's worth trying to find them, since they give a fantastic crisp texture. Ordinary dried white breadcrumbs can, of course, be substituted.

1 x 3 lb. sea bass, filleted

12 ounces fresh crabmeat

3 tablespoons well-flavored mayonnaise

1 red serrano chile, seeded and chopped

1 green jalapeño chile, seeded and chopped

1/2 teaspoon ground mace

2 tablespoons chopped cilantro leaves

6 tablespoons panko crumbs (see Hot Tip) or dried white breadcrumbs

1/3 cup olive oil

1 lb. fresh spinach

Salt and freshly ground black pepper

For the red pepper chutney:

1 onion, chopped

2 garlic cloves, crushed

1 tablespoon olive oil

2 roasted red peppers, peeled and cut into strips 1/2 inch thick

1 teaspoon finely chopped fresh ginger root

1 teaspoon seeded and finely chopped New Mexican chile

1/2 cup red wine vinegar

1/4 cup brown sugar

2 tablespoons raisins

1/2 cup tomato sauce

For the sauce:

1 cup well-flavored chicken stock

1 inch piece of fresh ginger root, grated

2 lemongrass stalks, outer layers removed, shredded

3 tablespoons olive oil

Roasted salmon
with fennel, zucchini, and romesco sauce

Until relatively recently, salmon was an expensive fish. Now it's cheap enough to use often, and I love experimenting with it. Spices go well with salmon because they cut the richness. Here the tangy bite of the Spanish romesco sauce is a particularly good match.

For the romesco sauce, soak the roasted chiles in hot water for 30 minutes, then drain. Put the tomatoes in a saucepan and cook over medium heat until almost all the liquid has evaporated. Remove from the heat and let cool. Place the chile, roasted pepper, garlic, tomato paste, almonds, and bread in a blender, add the tomatoes, and blitz until smooth. Slowly add the lemon juice and oil while the machine is running. Season to taste.

Place the salmon fillets in a shallow dish. Mix the oil, herb stalks, and garlic together and pour them over the salmon, then let marinate at room temperature for 1 hour.

Preheat the oven to 400°F. Place the fennel in a large pot, cover with water, and bring to a boil. Simmer for 4–5 minutes, until tender, then drain. Heat an ovenproof frying pan, clean the marinated salmon of its herbs, and fry, skin-side up, for 1 minute or until golden. Turn it over, then place in the oven to roast for 5–8 minutes, until crisp.

Meanwhile, heat the butter in a frying pan, add the zucchini and fry for 4–5 minutes, until lightly golden. Add the fennel and black olives and season to taste.

Arrange the vegetables on 4 serving plates, top with the roasted salmon, and pour over them the romesco sauce. Garnish with the fresh herbs.

4 x 5 ounce salmon fillets (skin on)

1/4 cup olive oil

1 tablespoon cilantro leaves (reserve the stalks)

1 tablespoon small basil leaves (reserve the stalks)

1 garlic clove, crushed

8 baby fennel bulbs, trimmed

1/2 stick (1/4 cup) sweet butter

2 zucchini, thickly sliced

8 black olives, pitted and cut in half

Salt and freshly ground black pepper

For the romesco sauce:

2 dried De Arbol chiles, roasted (see p.8)

1/2 lb. ripe tomatoes (about 2 small to medium ones), skinned, seeded, and coarsely chopped

1 red pepper, roasted, peeled and chopped

2 garlic cloves, crushed

2 teaspoons tomato paste

1/3 cup blanched almonds, toasted

1 slice of white bread, crusts removed

2 tablespoons lemon juice

1/3 cup olive oil

Chili-roasted salmon
crisp vegetables and fragrant coconut rice

Preheat the oven to 350°F. First prepare the dressing by mixing all the ingredients together. Set aside.

Dust the salmon liberally with the chili powder and some salt. Heat a little oil in an ovenproof frying pan, place the salmon in it skin-side down and cook for 1 minute. Turn the fish over, transfer to the oven, and cook for 4–5 minutes, until just done.

Heat the cooked rice in a pan with the lemongrass and coconut cream, then season to taste. Pack into 4 buttered ramekins and keep warm.

For the vegetables, heat the butter and sesame oil in a large frying pan, add all the vegetables and the garlic, and stir-fry for 2–3 minutes, until crisp.

To serve, unmold the rice timbales on to 4 individual serving plates and top with the salmon. Arrange the stir-fried vegetables on top. Mix all the ingredients for the dressing together until the mixture is creamy. Pour the dressing around the salmon and serve immediately.

4 x 6 ounce salmon fillets (skin on)

2 tablespoons chili powder

A little oil for frying

1 cup cooked basmati rice

2 lemongrass stalks, outer layers removed, very finely chopped

1/2 cup unsweetened coconut cream

Salt and freshly ground black pepper

For the dressing:

2 tablespoons light soy sauce

2 shallots, finely chopped

1/4 cup rice vinegar

1 tablespoon plus 1 teaspoon sesame oil

1 tablespoon sugar

1/2 inch piece of fresh ginger root, finely chopped

11/2 small red chiles, seeded and chopped

2 tablespoons chopped cilantro

For the crisp vegetables:

2 tablespoons butter

2 tablespoons sesame oil

1/4 red pepper, cut into thin strips

1/4 yellow pepper, cut into thin strips

1 small pak choi, shredded

6 red radishes, thinly sliced

1 cup bean sprouts

4 ounces (a heaped cup) shiitake mushrooms, quartered

1 garlic clove, crushed

Grilled salmon trout
with a horseradish crust and beet vinaigrette

These crisp salmon trout fillets are accompanied by broiled zucchini, and leeks here, but I also like to serve them on a bed of creamy mashed potato flavored with puréed corn.

Cover the salmon trout fillets with a large piece of plastic wrap and lightly flatten them out into neat cutlets about 1/2 inch thick, using a meat bat or a rolling pin.

In a shallow container, mix together the horseradish, smoked salmon, dill, breadcrumbs, and a little salt and pepper. Season the salmon trout cutlets with salt and pepper and squeeze a little lemon juice over them. Dip the cutlets into the melted butter, then into the breadcrumb mixture on one side. Brush off any excess crumbs, then place in a well-buttered broiler pan, crumb-side up. Chill until required.

For the dressing, mix all the ingredients together and season to taste.

Preheat the broiler to a medium setting (or use a ridged grill pan). Toss the zucchini and leeks with the oil and some seasoning, and cook them under the broiler until golden and tender. Keep warm. Place the salmon trout under the broiler to cook for about 3–4 minutes, until the crumbs are crisp and golden in color.

To serve, put the broiled zucchini and leeks on 4 serving plates, top with the salmon trout, and pour the dressing around them.

4 x 6 ounce salmon trout fillets, skinned

2 tablespoons grated horseradish root

2 ounces smoked salmon, very finely chopped

1 tablespoon chopped dill

1 cup panko crumbs (see Hot Tip on p.47) or dried white breadcrumbs

Lemon juice

3/4 stick (1/3 cup) sweet butter, melted

2 zucchini, cut into slices 1/4 inch thick

12 baby leeks, trimmed

1/4 cup olive oil

Salt and freshly ground black pepper

For the beet vinaigrette:

1 red pepper, roasted, peeled and finely diced

1 small beet, cooked, peeled, and finely diced

1 shallot, finely diced

Zest of 1/2 lemon

1 tablespoon superfine capers, rinsed and drained

1/4 teaspoon saffron strands, steeped in 2 tablespoons boiling water

1 tablespoon chopped dill

6 tablespoons plain vinaigrette dressing of your choice

Chili-salt-baked red mullet
with orange–paprika oil

This simple-tasting dish is good served on a fresh tomato salad or with buttery couscous. Baking the mullet in salt seals in all the wonderful juices, so it emerges moist and succulent.

Preheat the oven to 400°F. Place a layer of about half the chili salt in a large baking pan and put the cleaned mullet on top.
Sprinkle the rosemary over it and lay 1 bay leaf on each fish. Completely cover the mullet with the remaining chili salt and then bake for 25 minutes.

Meanwhile mix all the ingredients for the oil together until you have a smooth emulsion. Remove the fish from the oven and let rest for 5 minutes. Carefully remove the salt from around the fish, and discard. Transfer the mullet to a serving dish and drizzle the oil over it.

HOT TIP In Indonesia and Malaysia, chili salt is available ready prepared. It is well worth trying to find some but it is also very simple to prepare at home. Just toast 10 De Arbol chiles in a hot frying pan for 20 seconds to release their fragrance. Place in a spice mill or coffee grinder and blitz to a fine powder, then mix with 1 lb. fine sea salt, or kosher salt. Store in an airtight container for about a week before using, so the salt becomes permeated with the chile.

1 lb. chili salt (see Hot Tip)
4 x 14 ounce red mullet, cleaned, fins and tails removed
4 rosemary sprigs, roughly chopped
4 bay leaves
For the orange–paprika oil:
1/2 cup virgin olive oil
2 teaspoons hot Hungarian paprika
1 tablespoon cilantro leaves
Juice of 2 oranges and zest of 1
2 teaspoons Harissa (see p.156)
Salt and freshly ground black pepper

Grilled red mullet
with fried tomatoes and rocket gribiche

Here peppery rocket leaves are complemented by a piquant dressing containing capers, gherkins and mustard. Both make a good foil for the oily-textured red mullet.

For the gribiche, separate the egg yolks and the whites and chop the whites into small dice. Put the yolks in a bowl with the mustard and gradually whisk in 100ml (31/2fl oz) of the olive oil, as if making mayonnaise. Add the capers, gherkins and egg white, then the parsley and shallots. Heat the vinegar and add to the sauce, then adjust the seasoning. Set aside.
Preheat the grill to its highest setting. Season the fish fillets with salt and pepper and squeeze over a little lemon juice. Arrange on an oiled grill pan, and

cook for 2–3 minutes on each side. While the fish is cooking, heat the remaining oil in a frying pan. Add the garlic and cook for 10 seconds to infuse, then add the tomatoes slices and fry for 1 minute on each side, until lightly coloured. Top with the basil, season and remove.
To serve, arrange the tomato slices on individual serving plates and stack 2 red mullet fillets on top. Dress the rocket leaves with the gribiche and place a mound of the salad by the side of the fish. Serve immediately.

2 eggs, hard-boiled
1 teaspoon Dijon mustard
165ml (5 1/2fl oz) olive oil
11/2 teaspoons fine capers
11/2 teaspoons small gherkins
1 tablespoon chopped parsley
2 shallots, finely chopped
2 tablespoons red wine vinegar
8 x 75g (3oz) red mullet fillets
Lemon juice
2 garlic cloves, crushed
4 beefsteak tomatoes, cut into slices
2 tablespoons roughly chopped basil
A good handful of small rocket leaves
Salt and freshly ground black pepper

GRILLED RED MULLET WITH FRIED TOMATOES

Asian blackened monkfish
with pickled vegetables and mint labna

This dish combines Eastern spicing with monkfish and labna, a Middle Eastern yoghurt cheese. The minted cheese is cool and refreshing against the fiery heat of the pickled vegetables. The vegetables also make a wonderful vegetarian dish served with rice.

For the labna, line a small strainer with a double layer of dampened cheesecloth, and put it over a bowl. Put the yoghurt in the strainer, then tie up the ends of the cheesecloth and leave overnight to drain. The next day, mix the yoghurt with the lemon and mint.

For the pickled vegetables, heat half the oil in a deep frying pan or in a large pot, add all the vegetables, and fry until golden. Remove from the pan and drain well. Heat the remaining oil in a heavy large pot, throw in the cumin, fenugreek, and curry leaves, and remove from the heat. After 1 minute,

add the garlic and chili powder and return to the heat. Now add the tomato paste, a little salt and pepper, and the fried vegetables. Reduce the heat and cook for 5–10 minutes, then stir in the sugar and vinegar. Remove from the heat and keep warm.

Season the fish liberally with the spice mix. Heat the oil in a large frying pan, then add the butter. Sear the fish in the hot fat on all sides for about 5–8 minutes, until golden brown.

To serve, divide the pickled vegetables between 4 serving plates, and place in a mound. Arrange the monkfish on top, then pour the labna around the fish.

4 x 6 ounce monkfish (angler fish) fillets
1/4 cup Asian blackened spice
* mix (p.156)*
3 tablespoons olive oil
1/2 stick (1/4 cup) sweet butter
For the mint labna:
2/3 cup yoghurt
Juice and zest of 1/4 lemon
1 tablespoon chopped mint
For the pickled vegetables:
1/2 cup vegetable oil
1 sweet potato, peeled and cut into
* 1/4 inch dice*
2 ounces pearl onions, peeled
1 small cauliflower, cut into
* small flowerets*
1 zucchini, cut into 1/4 inch dice
1/2 teaspoon cumin seeds
1/4 teaspoon fenugreek seeds
2 curry leaves, shredded
2 garlic cloves, crushed
1 teaspoon chili powder
1 tablespoon tomato paste
A pinch of sugar
1/4 cup vinegar
Salt and freshly ground black pepper

HOT TIP The pickled vegetables can be prepared in advance and kept in the fridge for 2–3 days, or longer if you bottle them in a sterilised jar. However, they will become spicier. Since I love hot food, I prefer them this way – the choice is yours!

Parsee monkfish curry
with mashed lentils and poppadom chips

The Parsees originate from Persia but settled in Bombay over a thousand years ago. Their cooking has a distinctive character, with hot/sour/sweet combinations and plenty of chiles. The sauces tend to be thick and savory, and very fragrant.

Place the garlic and ginger in a blender with 1/2 cup of water and blitz to a paste. Heat a small frying pan over high heat, add the whole spices and chili flakes, and toast them for 1 minute to release their fragrance. Place in a spice mill or coffee grinder and blitz to a fine powder. Add the turmeric and ground cloves and set aside.

Heat the vegetable oil in a large frying pan, then add the onion and fry until golden. Add the garlic-ginger paste and cook for 2 minutes, then stir in the ground spices. Add the monkfish and cook for 2–3 minutes. Stir in the tomatoes and 11/4 cups of water and bring to a boil.

Cover and simmer for 5–8 minutes, then remove the monkfish with a slotted spoon.

Add the cooked lentils, sugar, and lemon juice to the pan and cook for 10–15 minutes, then mash the lentils with a spoon to give a chunky texture. Stir in the coconut milk and return the monkfish to the sauce. Cook for a further 10 minutes, then adjust the seasoning and garnish with the freshly chopped mint and cilantro.

To make the poppadom chips, cut the poppadoms into 2 inch pieces, arrange them on a plate, and place in a microwave for about 1 minute.

Serve the chips immediately, with the fish curry.

2 garlic cloves, peeled

1 inch piece of fresh ginger root

1 teaspoon cumin seeds

1/2 teaspoon cardamom seeds

1/2 teaspoon black peppercorns

1 teaspoon dried red chili flakes

1 teaspoon ground turmeric

1/2 teaspoon ground cloves

1/4 cup vegetable oil

1 onion, finely chopped

11/2 lbs. monkfish (angler fish) tail fillet,
*   cut into 2 inch pieces*

7 ounces canned tomatoes, crushed

11/4 cups cooked red lentils

1 teaspoon dark brown sugar

Juice of 1/2 lemon

1/2 cup coconut milk

Chopped mint and cilantro, for
*   garnishing*

8 spicy poppadoms

Salt and freshly ground black pepper

Spicy Moroccan sea bream
with garlic, raisin, and almond stuffing

This stuffing is sweet and moist, with a little spiciness typical of Moroccan cooking. In true Moroccan tradition, I have used raisins here but I have also tried it with dates, which worked equally well.

For the stuffing, cook the rice in a pot of boiling salted water for 45–50 minutes or until tender. Drain in a colander and let cool. Heat the butter in a large pan, add the onion and garlic, and cook over low heat until softened. Increase the heat, add the cooked rice, allspice, and harissa, and toss to coat the rice with the spices. Cook for 2–3 minutes, stir-frying the mixture a little. Place in a bowl, add the raisins, pine nuts, ground almonds, and cilantro and let cool.

Stir in the beaten egg and season to taste.

Preheat the oven to 400°F. Slash the fish 3 times on each side and then season inside and outside with salt and pepper. Fill the cavity with the spicy rice stuffing, packing it in well, then place the fish in a large baking pan, squeeze the lemon juice over it, and pour in the oil. Place in the oven for 20–25 minutes, until the fish is cooked. Serve with a little olive oil drizzled over the fish and accompanied by the lemon wedges.

HOT TIP With its wonderful color, Camargue red rice is definitely destined to be a fashionable ingredient. It is an unpolished wholegrain rice from the Camargue area of France. You should be able to find it in large supermarkets and delicatessens.

1 x 3 lb. sea bream, cleaned and
  gutted
Juice of 1 lemon
6 tablespoons olive oil, plus a little extra
  for serving
1 lemon, cut into wedges
Salt and freshly ground black pepper

For the stuffing:

3/4 cup Camargue red rice (see Hot
  Tip), washed
1/2 stick (1/4 cup) sweet butter
1 onion, finely chopped
2 garlic cloves, crushed
1/2 teaspoon ground allspice
1 teaspoon Harissa (see p.156)
1/2 cup raisins, soaked in a little hot
  water for 20 minutes and then drained
1/2 cup pine nuts, toasted
2 tablespoons ground almonds
1/4 cup chopped cilantro
1 egg, lightly beaten

Cajun turbot
with wilted greens, butternut squash, and Creole vinaigrette

This wonderful mustardy vinaigrette is very versatile. I like to use it on leaf salads or tossed with hot vegetables such as green beans or tomatoes.

For the Creole vinaigrette, mix all the ingredients together and let stand for at least 30 minutes before use.

Heat the butter and half the oil in a large frying pan and add the squash, mixed greens, and 1/4 cup of water. Cover and cook over high heat for about 8–10 minutes, until the vegetables are tender. Add the corn and heat through briefly. Season with salt and pepper and keep it warm while you prepare the fish.

Dust the turbot fillets all over with the spice mix. Heat the remaining oil in a large frying pan over high heat and add the turbot (it will give off a fair amount of smoke, which is indicative of a blackened dish). Cook until well browned, then turn the fish over and cook the other side. It will take about 4–5 minutes altogether, depending on thickness.

Arrange the vegetables on serving plates, top with the turbot, and pour the Creole vinaigrette around. Serve immediately.

HOT TIP When buying turbot fillet, always check that the flesh is not bruised. If it is, this indicates that the fish has not been bled properly, in which case it is unusable.

2 tablespoons sweet butter

1/4 cup olive oil

1/2 butternut squash, peeled, seeded and cut into wedges 1/4–1/2 inch thick

11/2 lbs. young mixed greens, such as kale, mustard greens, Swiss chard, and spinach

1/2 cup canned corn, drained

4 x 6 ounces turbot fillets

1/4 cup Blackened Cajun spice mix (see p.157)

Salt and freshly ground black pepper

For the Creole vinaigrette:

2 tablespoons red wine vinegar

1/2 cup olive oil

2 teaspoons coarse grain mustard

2 shallots, finely chopped

1 red jalapeño chile, seeded and finely diced

1 red pepper, roasted, peeled and finely diced

1 teaspoon lemon juice

Chargrilled John Dory
with tomatoes, fennel, and chile and arugula salsa verde

John Dory can be difficult to find unless you are lucky enough to have a good-quality fish market locally. It is best during the late summer and early autumn, which is the ideal time to prepare this light and simple dish. If you do have a problem obtaining it, replace it with sole, turbot, or brill.

Warm the virgin olive oil in a shallow saucepan, add the fennel and bay leaf, and leave barely simmering for 10–15 minutes, until the fennel is just tender. Add the garlic cloves, tomato quarters, and olives, and let cook for a further 10 minutes.

Meanwhile, in a blender or food processor, blend all the ingredients for the salsa verde together. Season to taste, and set aside. Heat a ridged grill pan. Season the fish with cayenne, salt, and pepper, and cook on the grill for 3–4 minutes each side.

Drain the fennel and tomato mixture and place on 4 serving plates, then top with the chargrilled fish. Put the balsamic vinegar and meat stock in a small pan and bring to a boil, then whisk in 2 tablespoons of the oil from cooking the vegetables. Adjust the seasoning.

To serve, top the fish with a spoonful of the spicy salsa verde and pour a little of the sauce around it.

1/2 cup virgin olive oil

2 fennel bulbs, trimmed and cut
   into wedges

1 bay leaf

8 garlic cloves, peeled

8 plum tomatoes, quartered

12 green olives, pitted

2 lbs. John Dory fillet, skinned
   and cut into 12 sticks

A pinch of cayenne pepper

2 tablespoons balsamic vinegar

1/2 cup meat stock

Salt and freshly ground black pepper

For the salsa verde:

1/4 cup arugula leaves

2 tablespoons basil leaves

2 tablespoons flat-leaf parsley

1/4 cup superfine capers, rinsed
   and drained

1 garlic clove, crushed

1 tablespoon balsamic vinegar

1 tablespoon Dijon mustard

1 green jalapeño chile, seeded
   and chopped

1/4 cup olive oil

Adobado grilled snapper
with curly fennel and radish ceviche

Adobado is the Mexican term for a meat or fish dish that has been marinated in a punchy, spicy-sour mixture. It should not be confused with an adobo, which uses a similar marinade but is more of a stew.

For the ceviche, I like to use my favorite oriental radishes, which are a stunning red or green color. Available in Chinese grocery stores, they are well worth seeking out. Mooli (daikon) or ordinary red radishes may be substituted, of course.

Preheat the broiler to its highest setting. Place the chiles on the broiler pan and toast them lightly under the broiler for about 10 seconds – be careful they do not burn. Open up the chiles and return them to the broiler to toast the insides. Place them in a blender with the garlic, scallions, vinegar, orange juice, cumin seeds, herbs, and water, and blitz to a smooth purée.

Heat the vegetable oil in a saucepan, add the adobado mixture and the brown sugar, and fry for 5–6 minutes, until the oil comes to the surface and the sauce has reduced. Transfer to a large bowl and let cool.

Meanwhile, prepare the ceviche. Discard the fronds and outer layers of the fennel, take off any stringy bits with a vegetable peeler, and then cut each bulb in half vertically. Shred very thinly, preferably on a mandoline, and place in a bowl of iced water for about 20 minutes to curl up. Trim the radishes, shred them thinly, and place in the iced water, too.

Drain the fennel and radishes and place them in a bowl. Add the leaves from the cilantro and toss together. Season with salt and pepper, then add the oil, lime juice, and garlic, and let marinate for 20 minutes.

Marinate the snapper fillets in the adobado mixture for 15 minutes, then broil for 3–4 minutes on each side under a broiler or on a ridged grill pan. Spoon over them a little of the oil from the adobado. To serve, put the ceviche on individual serving plates and top with the grilled snapper.

1 chipotle chile

1 ancho chile

2 garlic cloves, chopped

2 scallions, chopped

2 tablespoons red wine vinegar

3 tablespoons fresh orange juice

1/2 teaspoon cumin seeds

1 teaspoon dried oregano, preferably Mexican

1/2 teaspoon dried thyme

1/3 cup water

6 tablespoons vegetable oil

2 tablespoons brown sugar

4 x 6 ounce snapper fillets

For the ceviche:

2 fennel bulbs

1 red oriental radish

1 green oriental radish

A bunch of fresh cilantro

1/4 cup olive oil

1/4 cup lime juice

1 garlic clove, crushed

Salt and freshly ground black pepper

Sugar-seared tuna
with sticky rice cakes, choi sum, and ginger–lime ponzu

Marinating fish in brown sugar or palm sugar is a favorite trick of mine as it gives it a beautifully caramelized exterior. Ponzu, a Japanese dipping sauce used for sashimi, sushi, and other dishes, makes a good, tart contrast. It is very simple to prepare and wonderfully tasty. A word of advice would be to make a large amount of it, since you'll find yourself looking for more – it really is good! Try it with all types of grilled seafood.

To make the marinade, gently heat the sugar in a pan until dissolved, then add 2/3 cup of water and bring to a boil. Boil for 2 minutes, until sticky in consistency. Add the nam pla and chile sauce and cook for 1 minute, then pour into a bowl. Stir in the garlic, ginger, and lime juice and let cool. Place the tuna steaks in the marinade, turning to coat them, and leave for 2 hours.

In a bowl, combine the cooked rice with 4 of the scallions and shape into 4 patties, about 3 inches in diameter and 3/4 inch high.

Steam the choi sum and season with half the sesame oil and some salt and pepper. Keep warm.

Heat the vegetable oil in a large frying pan until almost smoking. Remove the tuna from the marinade, add to the pan, and fry quickly for about 1 minute on each side, until browned and caramelized. Remove from the pan and keep warm.

Fry the scallion cakes in the remaining sesame oil until golden and crisp.

For the ponzu, simply place all the ingredients in a pan and bring to boiling point, then remove from the heat.

To serve, arrange a scallion cake on each serving plate, drape the choi sum over them, and top with the caramelized tuna. Sprinkle the ponzu dressing on top, along with the remaining scallions, and serve immediately.

4 x 7 ounces tuna fillets

3 cups cooked sushi rice (or other glutinous rice)

6 scallions, finely shredded

12 ounces choi sum (Chinese flowering cabbage)

2 tablespoons sesame oil

1/4 cup vegetable oil

For the marinade:

1/4 cup brown sugar

1 tablespoon nam pla (Thai fish sauce)

1 tablespoon sweet chile sauce

1 garlic clove, crushed

1 inch piece of fresh ginger root, finely grated

Juice of 1/2 lime

For the ginger–lime ponzu:

Juice of 1 lime

2 tablespoons rice vinegar

11/2 inch piece of fresh ginger root, finely chopped

2 tablespoons dark soy sauce

1 tablespoon mirin (Japanese sweet rice wine)

1/2 cup well-flavored chicken stock

1 tablespoon chopped cilantro

Sri Lankan stir-fried squid
with garlic and ginger paste

Rice and stir-fried greens make good accompaniments to this simple dish.

Place the onion, garlic, ginger, and chiles in a blender or food processor and blitz to a smooth paste. Heat 1/2 cup of the olive oil in a pan, add the paste, and cook over low heat for 10–12 minutes, until aromatic and golden. Add the spice mix and cook for 5 minutes, then stir in the coconut milk and 2/3 cup of water and bring to a boil. Reduce the heat and simmer for a further 10–15 minutes, until the sauce has thickened slightly.

Heat the remaining oil in a wok or large frying pan over high heat. Add the squid and stir-fry for 1 minute to seal. Add the sauce and toss together for 1 minute, then serve.

1 onion, roughly chopped
2 garlic cloves, crushed
1 inch piece of fresh ginger root, roughly chopped
2 red Thai chiles, chopped
2/3 cup olive oil
2 tablespoons Sri Lankan spice mix (see p.157)
2/3 cup coconut milk
1 lb. cleaned young squid, tentacles left whole, body cut into rings

Seafood gumbo

Gumbo is a much-loved speciality of Louisiana, a great soup for those with big appetites, I think it makes a hearty main course too, which explains the large quantities in this recipe.

Scrub the mussels and clams under cold running water, removing the beards from the mussels and discarding any open mussels or clams that don't close when tapped on a work surface. Put them in a large pot, cover with the chicken stock and bring to a boil. Cook over high heat for about 2–3 minutes, shaking the pot occasionally, until the mussels and clams open. Drain in a colander and strain the stock through a fine mesh strainer. Shell the mussels and clams, discarding the shells.

Heat the oil in a heavy pan, then stir in the flour to make a roux. Stir constantly over a medium-high heat until it turns a deep brown (about the color of peanut butter); this will take about 10–15 minutes. Add the onion, green pepper, and celery, reduce the heat, and cook gently for 5 minutes. Add the sausage, tomatoes, and garlic, and whisk in the reserved stock a little at a time. Add the scallions and bring to a boil, stirring frequently. Stir in the Worcestershire sauce and simmer for 40 minutes, skimming off the fat that rises to the top.

Add the mussels, clams, shrimp, and crabmeat to the soup and cook for 5 minutes. Season with salt and Tabasco to taste, then serve.

1 lb. mussels
1 lb. venus clams
1 1/2 quarts well-flavored chicken stock
1/4 cup vegetable oil
1/2 cup all purpose flour
1 onion, chopped
1 green pepper, chopped
1 celery stalk, chopped
2 ounces andouille or chorizo sausage, sliced
2 small to medium tomatoes, diced
1 garlic clove, crushed
6 scallions, shredded
1 tablespoon Worcestershire sauce
1 lb. large raw tiger shrimp, peeled and de-veined
4 ounces (about 1/2 cup) crabmeat
Tabasco sauce
Salt

Cioppino
(seafood stew)

From the Italian community of San Francisco, this is similar to the classic fish stews of Italy, fired up with a little dried chile. It's a great winter dish, best served with chunks of bread for dipping. Use any mixture of fish and shellfish you can lay your hands on.

Scrub the mussels and clams under cold running water, removing the beards from the mussels and discarding any open mussels or clams that don't close when tapped on a work surface.

Heat half the olive oil in a saucepan, add the garlic, shallots, and fennel, and cook gently until golden. Add the white wine and simmer until reduced by half. Add the tomato sauce and both fish and chicken stocks. Bring to a boil, then add the herbs and chili flakes and simmer over low heat for 15 minutes.

Meanwhile, cut the snapper fillet into diamonds, then sauté in the remaining oil in a large pot until golden brown on both sides. Add the mussels, clams, shrimp, and squid. Pour in the tomato broth and increase the heat. Cover, and cook until the clams and mussels open. Season to taste, then transfer to a large soup tureen and serve.

1 lb. mussels
1 lb. clams
1/4 cup olive oil
1 garlic clove, crushed
2 shallots, chopped
1 fennel bulb, finely diced
1/2 cup white wine
1/3 cup tomato sauce
2/3 cup fish stock
2/3 cup chicken stock
1 tablespoon chopped mixed herbs,
  such as parsley, chervil, and basil
1/2 teaspoon dried red chili flakes
12 ounces red snapper fillet
12 large raw tiger shrimp, peeled and
  de-veined
5 ounces small squid, cut into pieces
Salt and freshly ground black pepper

Tiger shrimp, tomato, and date curry

I picked up this recipe during a stint working in Singapore, where it is usually made with lobster. Traditionally the red dates unique to the area are used, but it is just as good with ordinary dates.

Heat a large frying pan or a wok over high heat, add half the oil, then season the shrimp with a little salt and pepper and throw them into the pan. Stir-fry for 2–3 minutes, then remove from the pan and set aside.

Heat the remaining oil in the pan, add the green pepper and chiles, and stir-fry for 1 minute. Stir in the curry paste and cook for 2 minutes or until fragrant. Add the coconut cream, the fish sauce, sugar, tomatoes, and dates, reduce the heat and cook slowly for 5–8 minutes, stirring occasionally. Finally, return the shrimp to the sauce and cook for a further minute.

Put the curry in a serving dish and sprinkle with the chopped cilantro. Serve with fluffy, steamed white rice.

1/3 cup vegetable oil
32 large raw tiger shrimp, peeled
  and de-veined
1 green pepper, cut into 1/2 inch dice
2 red Thai chiles, thinly sliced
3 tablespoons curry paste
11/2 cups unsweetened coconut
  cream
2 tablespoons nam pla (Thai fish sauce)
2 tablespoons sugar
1 lb. small tomatoes (about 4), skinned
  and chopped
12 fresh dates, pitted and cut in half
1 tablespoon chopped cilantro
Salt and freshly ground black pepper

Shrimp piri-piri

Piri-piri is the name of a hot chile and also of this classic sauce, originally from Portuguese Africa. It can be searingly hot, so approach with caution.

Place the chiles, 2/3 cup of the oil, the garlic, and lemon juice in a blender, and blitz to a purée. Heat the remaining oil in a large frying pan, season the shrimp with a little salt and paprika, and fry for 1–2 minutes until cooked. Add the jalapeño purée, blend together, and cook for 1 minute. Serve immediately, sprinkled with the parsley and accompanied by steamed rice.

HOT TIP Leave a little of the tail shell on the prawns for an attractive presentation.

*8 red jalapeño chiles, seeded and
  chopped*

3/4 cup olive oil

2 garlic cloves, chopped

Juice of 1 lemon

*24 large raw tiger shrimp, peeled and
  de-veined*

Smoked paprika

1 tablespoon chopped parsley

Salt

* Goan red masala lobster

I could live on this dish seven days a week. Like much of Goan cuisine, it is hot, sweet, and fragrant. Scottish lobsters have the finest flavor, so do use these if you can find them. Basmati rice, plainly steamed or flavored with turmeric, makes the best accompaniment.

First make the masala: toast the coriander and cumin seeds in a hot pan, then place them in a spice mill or coffee grinder and blitz to a fine powder. Put the coconut cream, turmeric, ginger, garlic, and chili powder in a blender with 2/3 cup of water and purée until smooth. Add the ground seeds and set aside.

Heat the vegetable oil in a large frying pan, add the onion, and cook until golden. Pour in the prepared masala and cook over medium heat until the liquid has evaporated and the oil has separated from the spice mixture. Cook for a further 10–15 minutes, then add another 2/3 cup of water, and simmer over medium heat until the mixture has reduced by about a quarter in volume. Add the tomatoes, tomato paste, garam masala, and lobster.

Season to taste and cook for 3–4 minutes to heat through. Sprinkle with the chopped cilantro and served accompanied by the lime wedges.

HOT TIP It is very easy to make your own garam masala. Just mix together 4 teaspoons of freshly ground cardamom and 1 teaspoon each of freshly ground cinnamon, cloves, cumin, and black pepper. Store in an airtight container.

2 tablespoons vegetable oil

1 onion, finely chopped

4 plum tomatoes, skinned, seeded and roughly chopped

2 teaspoons tomato paste

1/2 teaspoon garam masala (see Hot Tip)

4 x 11/2 lb. cooked lobsters, preferably Scottish, cut into sections, claws cracked

2 tablespoons chopped cilantro

1 lime, cut into wedges

Salt and freshly ground black pepper

For the masala:

2 teaspoons coriander seeds

2 teaspoons cumin seeds

1/2 packet of unsweetened coconut cream

1 teaspoon ground turmeric

2 inch piece of fresh ginger root, chopped

4 garlic cloves, crushed

1/2 teaspoon chili powder

poultry and meat

HONEY-ROASTED DUCK

Guinea fowl
with smoked sausages, cannellini beans, and mustard jus

Place the soaked cannellini beans in a pot, cover with plenty of cold water, and bring to a boil. Simmer for 1 hour or until tender, then drain.

Preheat the oven to 400°F. Season the guinea fowl breasts with salt and pepper. Heat the oil in a large frying pan, add the guinea fowl, and cook, skin-side down, for 2–3 minutes, until golden. Remove from the pan and set aside.

Add the garlic, mushrooms, lardons, and sausages to the pan, and sauté over low heat until colored. Add the stock and cook for 10 minutes, then add the cannellini beans. Stir in the mustard and bay leaf, then transfer everything to a casserole dish. Top the beans with the guinea fowl, cover, and place in the oven for 20–25 minutes, until the guinea fowl is cooked.

Serve straight from the oven, accompanied by creamy mashed potatoes.

1 cup cannellini beans, soaked in
   water overnight and then drained

7 ounce guinea fowl breasts

1/4 cup vegetable oil

1 garlic clove, crushed

3 ounces wild mushrooms, cut up if large

3 ounce piece of smoked bacon or
   smoked ham, cut into lardons

4 smoked pork sausages, skinned and
   cut into slices

11/4 cups chicken stock

1 tablespoon tarragon mustard

1 bay leaf

Salt and freshly ground black pepper

Honey-roasted duck
with nutmeg and dried tangerine peel

I use nutmeg quite a lot in cooking. It has a subtle, scented heat. Cooking the duck in this way gives it a wonderful sweet, shiny glaze, similar to Peking duck. Serve with buttered Swiss chard, or with pak choi for a more authentic accompaniment.

Blanch the duck breasts in a large pot of boiling salted water for 2 minutes, then plunge them into a bowl of iced water. Remove and dry on a cloth.

In a blender, blitz together the honey or maple syrup, lime juice, olive oil, five-spice powder, and nutmeg. Coat the duck breasts in this mixture, then sprinkle with the Szechuan pepper and sear in a heavy frying pan over medium heat until well done (otherwise cook in a moderate oven for 15–20 min-

utes). The duck should be cooked slowly and become glazed and caramel-colored.

Remove the duck from the pan and keep warm. Add the balsamic vinegar, chicken stock, *ketjap manis*, ginger, chile, tangerine juice, and chopped dried peel to the pan. Bring to a boil and simmer until reduced and syrupy in consistency.

Cut the duck into neat slices, coat with the sauce, and serve.

HOT TIP Dried tangerine peel is available from oriental supermarkets and is also simple to prepare at home. Peel a tangerine and place the peel in a very low oven to dry for about 2 hours, until crisp. Chop finely and store in an airtight container.

4 x 8 ounce duck breasts

2 tablespoons honey or maple syrup

2 tablespoons lime juice

6 tablespoons olive oil

1 teaspoon five-spice powder

1/2 teaspoon grated nutmeg

1/2 teaspoon Szechuan pepper

1 tablespoon balsamic vinegar

21/2 cups well-flavored
   chicken stock

1/4 cup ketjap manis
   (Indonesian soy sauce)

1 inch piece of fresh ginger root,
   finely chopped

1 red Thai chile, thinly sliced

Juice and dried peel of 2 tangerines
   (see Hot Tip)

Braised duck legs in tamarind sauce
with roasted jalapeño sweet potatoes

Blitz together all the marinade ingredients in a blender. Place the duck legs in a bowl, then spread the blended spice mixture over them and let marinate for 2 hours.

Preheat the oven to 400°F. Heat the oil in a heavy flameproof casserole dish (or other flameproof and ovenproof pan). Remove the duck from the marinade and fry them in the hot oil until golden all over. Add the curry leaves and fenugreek seeds and fry for 1 minute. Add the marinade and 1¼ cups of water and mix well to form a sauce. Bring to a boil, then reduce the heat, cover, and transfer to the oven. Cook for 50–60 minutes or until the duck is tender.

Meanwhile, toss the sweet potatoes with the oil and green chile, season with salt and pepper, and roast in the oven for 25–30 minutes, until they are well caramelized.

Remove the duck casserole from the oven, stir in the red chile and cilantro, and adjust the seasoning. To serve, divide the sweet potatoes between 4 serving plates, top with the braised duck legs, and pour the sauce over them.

HOT TIP Tamarind is the pulp from the long, brown pods of the tamarind tree and has an intensely sour flavor. The most convenient form to buy it in is a paste – available from Indian and Asian grocery stores, large supermarkets, and some wholefood stores. But you can also buy blocks of compressed tamarind pods that have to be soaked in hot water and then squeezed out to extract the pulp.

4 large duck legs

1/4 cup vegetable oil

6 curry leaves

1 teaspoon fenugreek seeds

*1 red jalapeño chile, seeded and
  chopped*

3 tablespoons chopped cilantro

Salt and freshly ground black pepper

For the marinade:

1 tablespoon tamarind paste

1 red jalapeño chile, chopped

1 tablespoon tomato paste

1 teaspoon salt

1 tablespoon sugar

*1 inch piece of fresh ginger root,
  chopped*

1 garlic clove, chopped

1/2 teaspoon ground cumin

1 teaspoon coriander seeds

For the sweet potatoes:

*1 lb. orange-fleshed sweet
  potatoes, peeled and cut into 3/4 inch
  dice*

1/4 cup olive oil

1 green jalapeño chile, thinly sliced

"Hot Morocco" chicken
with sweet spices and harissa

For the marinade, place all the ingredients in a blender and blitz to a smooth purée. Season the chicken pieces with a little salt and place them in a dish. Pour the marinade over them and mix well, then let marinate for about 2 hours. Remove the chicken from the marinade.

Heat the olive oil in a frying pan and fry the chicken breasts for 6–8 minutes, until golden, turning once. Mix the tomato paste with the chicken stock. Pour the marinade over the chicken, add the stock, and bring to a boil. Reduce the heat, then cover and cook for 8–10 minutes, until the sauce has reduced enough to coat the chicken. Serve sprinkled with the cilantro.

3 tablespoons olive oil

Juice of 1 lemon

2 garlic cloves, crushed

1/2 teaspoon whole aniseed

1/2 teaspoon ground cinnamon

1/2 teaspoon ground ginger

1 teaspoon ground cumin

1 teaspoon ground coriander

1/2 teaspoon paprika

1 red jalapeño chile, seeded and diced

11/2 teaspoons Harissa (see p.156)

For the chicken:

3 tablespoons olive oil

2 tablespoons cilantro leaves

1 tablespoon tomato paste

21/2 cups chicken stock

4 chicken breasts, boned and skinned

Salt

Sauté chicken Colombo

Serve this simple sauté with some fluffy white rice. I also like to have some fruit with it, such as pineapple, raisins, and mango. Serving fruit with spicy dishes is typical of Caribbean cookery. If you cannot find a Habenero chile, subsitute 1/2 teaspoon of West Indian hot pepper sauce.

Season the chicken pieces with salt, pepper, and 1 tablespoon of the spice mix, and leave for 2 hours.

Heat the oil in a large heavy pan, add the chicken and sauté until lightly golden in color; do not color too much. Pour off the excess fat, add the onion and garlic, and cook for 2 minutes. Stir in the remaining spice mix and cook over low heat for 2 minutes. Add the remaining vegetables, plus the chile and enough water just to cover the chicken. Bring to a boil, add the bay leaf, then reduce the heat, cover, and cook for 30–40 minutes, until the chicken is tender.

Stir in the lime juice, check the seasoning, and then serve immediately.

1 x 3 lb. chicken, cut into 8 pieces

3 tablespoons Colombo spice mix (see p.156) or mild curry powder

3 tablespoons vegetable oil

1 onion, chopped

3 garlic cloves, thinly sliced

4 scallions, shredded

1 large eggplant, cut into 3/4 inch dice

2 zucchini, cut into 3/4 inch dice

1 habanero chile, seeded and chopped

1 bay leaf

3 tablespoons lime juice

Salt and freshly ground black pepper

A simple Mediterranean spice-roasted chicken

Preheat the oven to 400°F. In a large bowl, mix together the cilantro, parsley, cumin seeds, paprika, turmeric, and some salt and pepper. Whisk in the oil, lemon juice, and harissa. Generously coat the chicken with the spice mixture and let marinate for 2 hours.

Roast in the oven for 1–11/4 hours (see Hot Tip for stuffing suggestion), until the chicken is golden all over and the juices run clear when a skewer is inserted near the thigh bone.

Let rest for 15 minutes before carving and serving. This dish is equally delicious served cold.

HOT TIP This is nice filled with a fruity couscous stuffing before roasting. Simply cook couscous in some stock to which a little saffron has been added, then mix in some chopped no-need-to-soak dried figs, prunes, and apricots, chopped cilantro leaves, and season to taste.

3 tablespoons chopped cilantro
3 tablespoons chopped flat-leaf parsley
1 tablespoon cumin seeds
11/2 teaspoons smoked paprika
1 teaspoon ground turmeric
2/3 cup olive oil
Juice of 1/2 lemon
2 tablespoons Harissa (see p.156)
1 x 31/2 lb. roasting chicken
Salt and freshly ground black pepper

✱ Fiery Keralan chicken

A hot southern Indian dish for real chile afficionados, flavored with fragrant spices.

Heat half of the ghee or oil in a frying pan, add the onion, and cook over gentle heat until golden. Put the onion in a blender or food processor along with the ginger, garlic, cumin, coriander, fenugreek, peppercorns, vinegar, and 1/2 teaspoon of salt. Blend until smooth, then transfer to a bowl and add the turmeric, sugar, curry leaves, cardamom pods, cinnamon, aniseed, and whole chiles.

Heat the remaining ghee or oil in a large heavy pan. Add the chicken pieces and fry for 10–12 minutes, until golden. Add the spice paste and increase the heat to seal the paste to the chicken. Add the tomato paste and the water or stock. Bring to a boil, reduce the heat, and simmer until the chicken is very tender, adding a little more water if necessary. Season to taste and then serve with rice.

1/4 cup ghee or vegetable oil
1 large onion, chopped
1 inch piece of fresh ginger root, chopped
4 garlic cloves, chopped
2 teaspoons cumin seeds
2 teaspoons coriander seeds
2 teaspoons fenugreek seeds
2 teaspoons black peppercorns
1/4 cup white wine vinegar
1 teaspoon ground turmeric
2 teaspoons sugar
4 curry leaves
10 fresh cardamom pods, cracked
1 teaspoon ground cinnamon
1 teaspoon whole aniseed
6 small De Arbol chiles
2 lbs. of chicken pieces, skinned
2 tablespoons tomato paste
11/4 cups water or chicken stock
Salt and freshly ground black pepper

MEDITERRANEAN SPICE-ROASTED CHICKEN

Pollo verde
(chicken in Mexican-style green sauce)

This is an adaptation of a recipe from my good friend, Alicia De'Angeli, of the El Tajin restaurant in Mexico City, who visited the Lanesborough for a promotion on Mexican food. It is very good served with spinach and chargrilled corn.

Roast, peel, and seed the poblano chiles (see page 8–9), then chop them finely and set aside.

Place the chicken breasts in a single layer in a large pan or flameproof casserole dish. Bring the stock to a boil and pour it over the chicken, then cook the chicken on a low simmer for 5–8 minutes. Remove the chicken breasts from the pan and set aside the stock.

Place the chiles, onion, herbs, sesame seeds, peanuts, tomatillos, tortillas, and lettuce leaves in a blender or food processor and purée until smooth. Heat the oil in a pan and add the purée. Cook for 5 minutes and then stir in the reserved chicken stock. Season with salt, add the chicken to the sauce and simmer for 5 minutes, basting with the sauce.

HOT TIP Tomatillos are an indispensable part of Mexican cooking. They look like pale green tomatoes with a papery, lantern-shaped husk. Unripe tomatoes can be used instead, although they lack the tart, citrussy flavor of tomatillos. Canned tomatillos are available from large delicatessens, while some specialist shops stock fresh ones occasionally.

2 green poblano chiles

4 chicken breasts, skinned

3 cups well-flavored chicken stock

1 onion, chopped

2 ounces cilantro leaves (a small bunch)

2 ounces flat-leaf parsley (a small bunch)

21/2 cups sesame seeds, toasted in a dry frying pan

1 tablespoon roasted peanuts

5 ounces fresh or canned tomatillos (or green tomatoes)

2 corn tortillas, chopped

8 romaine lettuce leaves, blanched in boiling water and then refreshed

2 tablespoons vegetable oil

Salt

foil-steamed baby chicken
in fragrant wasabi soy broth

A dish to keep dieters happy, since there is no added fat. It tastes clean and refreshing, and cooking the chicken in foil packages means that all the flavors are retained. I like to serve it with a little lemon and some fluffy white rice.

Preheat the oven to 400°F. Cut each chicken in half down the center. Season with a little salt, place in a dish, pour over them half the sake, and set aside.

Cut two 12 inch squares of aluminum foil and place a chicken halves on each piece. Put the vegetables on top of the chicken and bring up the edges of the foil carefully around the chicken.

Bring the chicken stock to a boil with the soy sauce, the remaining sake, and the lemon juice, then add the wasabi and remove from the heat.

Drizzle the flavored stock over the chicken and twist the edges of the foil together to make a close seal. Place both packages on a baking tray and place in the oven to steam for 20–25 minutes or until the chicken is cooked.

To serve, open the packages at the table to release the wonderful aroma.

2 x 18 ounce poussins, spatchcocked
(see Hot Tip)

1/4 cup sake (or dry sherry)

1 carrot, cut into thin strips

4 scallions, shredded

12 shiitake mushrooms, thinly sliced

2/3 cup chicken stock

6 tablespoons light soy sauce

1 tablespoon lemon juice

1/2 teaspoon wasabi paste

Salt

HOT TIP To spatchcock a bird, cut out the backbone with kitchen scissors or poultry shears. Break the wishbone, then turn the bird cut-side down and flatten it by pressing down with the heel of your hand. Turn it over and remove all the ribcage bones. An easier option is to buy the poussins ready-spatchcocked from a supermarket or good butcher's!

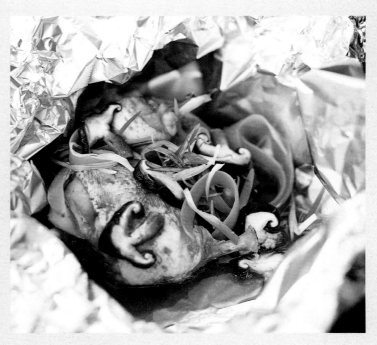

Braised chicken
with spiced lentils and peanut butter

Season the chicken liberally with salt and pepper. Heat the oil in a large, deep frying pan, add the chicken pieces, and cook until golden all over. Add the garlic, onion, and spices, and mix with the chicken. Reduce the heat and cook until the spices become fragrant. Add the lentils, carrots, and chicken stock, and bring to a boil, then stir in the berbere. Reduce the heat and simmer for 40–45 minutes, until the chicken and lentils are tender, skimming off any fat that rises to the surface.

Stir in the peanut butter, adjust the seasoning, and serve immediately.

1 x 3½ lb. chicken, cut into 8
3 tablespoons vegetable or peanut oil
1 garlic clove, crushed
1 onion, cut into ¼ inch dice
¼ teaspoon cayenne pepper
½ teaspoon ground cinnamon
½ teaspoon ground cloves
½ teaspoon fennel seeds
¾ cup Puy lentils
2 carrots, sliced
2½ cups chicken stock
2 teaspoons Ethiopian Berbere
  (see p.154)
¼ cup smooth peanut butter
Salt and freshly ground black pepper

Chocolate chile glazed pork

There have been many doubters about this recipe but I've won over a fair few of them, including food writer Sophie Grigson. Do give it a try. The flavors are fantastic, and not as outlandish as they at first appear.

Chocolate and chile are used a lot in Mexican cooking, resulting in a wonderful combination of sweetness and spice. I like to serve this with a fruity orange, red onion, and cucumber salad.

Preheat the oven to 375°F. Place the whole garlic cloves in a small baking pan, pour a little oil over them, and roast for 10–15 minutes, until soft and slightly charred. Let cool a little, then squeeze out the flesh.

Remove the stems and seeds from the ancho chiles. Soak the chiles in boiling water for 30 minutes, then drain. Place the chiles, achiote seeds, and roasted garlic flesh in a blender along with the herbs, vinegar, onion, and spices. Add enough water to blend to a smooth purée, then add the sugar and a little salt and pepper.

Trim the pork belly and smear the chile purée over it. Cover and refrigerate for at least 6–8 hours, preferably overnight.

Preheat the oven to 350°F. Remove the pork from the refrigerator and wipe off the excess chile purée. Place the pork in a baking pan, pour 1/2 cup of water around it, and cover with foil. Bake for 40–50 minutes, basting occasionally with the liquid. Remove the pork from the oven and cool slightly, discard the pan juices.

Blitz together all the ingredients for the glaze. Raise the oven heat to full, cut the pork into slices 1/4 inch thick, brush with the glaze, and return to the oven for about 10–12 minutes.

4 garlic cloves
A little oil
4 ancho chiles
1½ teaspoons achiote seeds
1 tablespoon cilantro leaves
1½ teaspoons fresh oregano
1 small bay leaf
½ cup white wine vinegar
½ small onion, chopped
A pinch each of ground cumin, cloves,
  and cinnamon
1 teaspoon sugar
1 lb., 10 oz. pork belly
Salt and freshly ground black pepper
For the glaze:
1 tablespoon honey, warmed
1 red chile, seeded and finely chopped
1 square unsweetened baking chocolate,
  melted

CHOCOLATE CHILLI GLAZED PORK

Chimichurri pork fillet

Chimichurri is a sort of Argentinian pesto, made with vinegar, oregano, garlic, and oil. It works well with any grilled fish or meat and is also very good in a sandwich of grilled vegetables. Traditionally it doesn't contain any chile but I prefer to include some. Be sure to use good-quality olive oil. Serve this dish with mashed potatoes and black beans.

Season the pork fillet with salt and pepper. Mix 1/4 cup of the oil with the garlic and chili powder, rub this mixture all over the pork fillet, and let marinate for 1 hour.

To make the chimichurri sauce, put all the ingredients in a blender and blitz to a coarse purée.

Heat the remaining oil in a frying pan, add the pork fillets, and fry for 3–4 minutes, turning them to give a wonderful golden color all over. Let them rest for a while, and then cut into thick slices.

Place on a serving dish, pour the chimichurri sauce over them, and serve.

4 x 7 ounce pieces of pork fillet
6 tablespoons olive oil
1 garlic clove, crushed
1 tablespoon chili powder
Salt and freshly ground black pepper
For the chimichurri sauce:
3 garlic cloves, crushed
A small bunch of cilantro
A small bunch of flat-leaf parsley
1 tablespoon fresh oregano (or
  1 teaspoon dried)
1 jalapeño chile, seeded and roughly
  chopped
2/3 cup olive oil
1/4 cup white wine vinegar

raised pork belly
vith Chinese spicy bean sauce

reheat the oven to 375°F. Season the pork liberal- with the five-spice powder and some salt and epper. Heat the oil in a flameproof casserole dish r other flameproof and ovenproof pan), add the ork, and seal it well all over, then remove and set ide. Add the lemongrass, ginger, garlic, onion, nd rice vinegar to the casserole dish and bring to boil. Then add the plum sauce, black bean sauce, ar anise, soy sauce, and chicken stock, and return to a boil.

Return the pork to the sauce, cover the casserole dish with a lid, and place in the oven to braise for 1–11/2 hours. Remove the pork from the sauce and keep it warm. Strain the sauce and keep warm.

For the garnish, heat the sesame oil in a wok or large frying pan, add the pak choi, garlic, and gin- ger, and stir-fry for 1 minute. Place in a serving dish. Slice the pork and place it on the pak choi. Pour the sauce over it and serve.

1 lb., 10 oz. pork belly

2 tablespoons five-spice powder

1/4 cup vegetable oil

3 lemongrass stalks, outer layers
    removed, chopped

2 inch piece of fresh ginger, chopped

1 garlic clove, crushed

1 onion, thinly sliced

2/3 cup rice vinegar

11/4 cups plum sauce

2 tablespoons Chinese spicy bean sauce

2 star anise

2 tablespoons soy sauce

3 tablespoons chicken stock

Salt and freshly ground black pepper

For the garnish:

1/4 cup sesame oil

1lb., 2 oz. pak choi

1 teaspoon crushed garlic

2 inch piece of fresh ginger,
    chopped

arbecue oregano-cured spare ribs

ike to serve this with steamed spring greens tossed with garlic and olive oil.

lace the chiles, onion, and garlic in a blender or od processor, and blitz to a purée. Add the chili owder, cumin, oregano, sugar, and vinegar, and end well. Rub the mixture into the spare ribs and t marinate overnight.

he next day, rub the olive oil over the spare ribs.

Place the spare ribs on a barbecue and cook for about 5 minutes on each side to seal all over, then move it to the edge of the grill (or raise the grill rack) to allow it to cook slowly for about 15–20 minutes. Let the meat rest for 10 minutes before serving.

OT TIP If your butcher hasn't French trimmed the spare ribs, here's how to do it: remove the skin, then cut way the layer of meat and fat from the top 2 inches of the bones. Clean the bones by scraping off all the maining bits of flesh.

8-bone spare ribs, French trimmed
    (see Hot Tip)

2 red serrano chiles, chopped

1 onion, chopped

4 garlic cloves, crushed

1 tablespoon chili powder

1 teaspoon ground cumin

2 teaspoons fresh oregano

2 tablespoons sugar

1 tablespoon white wine vinegar or
    cider vinegar

1/4 cup olive oil

Braised lamb kidneys
with chorizo, bacon, fava beans, and grain mustard polenta

For the polenta, put the milk and oil in a heavy pan and bring to a boil. Reduce to a simmer and then gradually rain in the polenta, stirring constantly. Reduce the heat and cook, stirring, for 15 minutes or until the polenta leaves the side of the pan. Stir in the Parmesan, butter, and cream, then the mustard. Season with salt and pepper and keep warm.

Peel the outer membrane off each kidney, cut them in half, and remove the central core. Heat the oil in a large frying pan, season the kidneys, and fry them in the hot oil for 3–4 minutes, until lightly col-ored. Remove from the pan and keep warm. Add the bacon lardons and chorizo to the pan and fry until lightly colored, then remove and set aside. Stir in the sherry and stock and simmer for 10 minutes, until the sauce reduces and thickens. Add the tarragon and whisk in the butter. Return all the meat to the sauce, along with the fava beans, and adjust the seasoning.

Put the mustard polenta on serving plates and top with the kidney mixture. Serve immediately.

12 lamb kidneys

1/4 cup vegetable oil

2 ounce slab of bacon, cut into lardons

5 ounces chorizo sliced 1/2 inch thick

1/2 cup sherry

21/2 cups meat stock

10 tarragon leaves

1 tablespoon sweet butter

a heaped 1/3 cup shelled fava beans (or, if unavailable, lima beans)

Salt and freshly ground black pepper

For the grain mustard polenta:

21/2 cups milk

3 tablespoons olive oil

12/3 cups polenta (or cornmeal)

21/2 cups finely grated Parmesan

1 stick (1/2 cup) sweet butter

1/2 cup heavy cream

2 tablespoons grain mustard

Red-cooked chargrilled lamb

A dish inspired by the cooking of Mexico's Yucatan peninsula, this uses a bright, richly flavored marinade based on the Hot achiote baste on page 146. It is very simple to prepare and ideal for a summer barbecue.

Put the chiles, garlic, onion, and achiote baste in a blender or food processor and blitz until smooth. Then add all the remaining ingredients except the lamb, and blitz again to make a marinade. Pour into a deep dish, immerse the lamb steaks in the marinade, and leave for 1–2 hours.

Remove the lamb from the dish and brush off any excess marinade. Place on a barbecue or ridged grill pan and cook for between 5 and 8 minutes on each side, until nicely chargrilled. Serve immediately with a Hot Mexican salsa (see page 151), if you like.

4 red jalapeño chiles, chopped

2 garlic cloves, chopped

1 small onion, chopped

1 tablespoon Hot achiote baste (see p.146)

2/3 cup fresh orange juice

1/2 cup tomato ketchup

1 teaspoon dried oregano

2 teaspoons Dijon mustard

2 tablespoons Worcestershire sauce

1/4 cup white wine vinegar

4 lamb leg steaks, cut horizontally from the leg, weighing 8–10 ounces each

Lamb sosaties
with tsire

Sosaties are South African kebabs, prepared with all kinds of meats. Their roots probably lie in Malaysian cuisine, since the name derives from the Malay word *sate*, or spiced sauce. Tsire is also South African, a mixture of ground peanuts, chili, and spices that is usually sprinkled over chargrilled meat. These sosaties are excellent served with couscous or tabbouleh.

Pat the lamb dry and place in a large bowl. Add the grated onion, garlic, ginger, coriander, curry powder, apricot jam, turmeric, and some salt and pepper. Scatter over it the chile and lemon zest, then pour in the vinegar and mix well. Cover with plastic wrap and chill for up to 6 hours.

Remove the meat from the marinade and thread on to 4 large skewers. Sprinkle over it the chopped bay leaves and grill or barbecue the skewers for 8–10 minutes, turning occasionally, until cooked.

Meanwhile, put the peanuts in a blender or food processor and blitz coarsely. Add the mixed spice, chili powder, and some salt, and blitz for 3 seconds, keeping the mixture like small niblets.

When the sosaties are cooked, transfer to a serving dish and scatter the tsire on top.

1 lb. lamb (leg or shoulder), cut
   into 1 inch cubes
1 onion, grated
2 garlic cloves, crushed
2 teaspoons ground ginger
2 teaspoons ground coriander
1 tablespoon curry powder
4 teaspoons apricot jam
1 teaspoon ground turmeric
1 serrano chile, seeded and finely
   chopped
1 teaspoon grated lemon zest
1 tablespoon white wine vinegar
2 bay leaves, finely chopped
Salt and freshly ground black pepper

For the tsire:
1/3 cup salted peanuts
1 teaspoon ground mixed spice
1 teaspoon chili powder
Salt

slow-cooked lamb shanks
with tchermila and spiced eggplant

Lamb shanks are given a Middle Eastern treatment in this dish, with a fragrant tchermila spice paste. As the name implies, this is very similar to the Moroccan chermoula. The paste can be kept in the fridge in an airtight container for 2 weeks or in the freezer for 1 month.

Place all the ingredients for the tchermila paste in a blender and blitz until smooth. Season the lamb shanks with salt, then rub them all over with the paste. Cover and let marinate for at least 2 hours, preferably 8 hours.

Preheat the oven to 300°F. Heat 3 tablespoons of the oil in a large flameproof casserole dish (or other flameproof and ovenproof pan) over high heat. Add the shanks and brown them all over for 6–8 minutes, then remove from the casserole dish. Add the remaining oil to the casserole dish, then throw in the onion, reduce the heat, and cook for 1 minute. Add the ginger, cinnamon, and tomatoes, and cook briefly to meld the flavors. Return the lamb shanks to the casserole dish and stir to mix with the spices and tomatoes. Pour over it the orange juice and stock or water, season with salt and pepper, and bring to a boil. Cover the casserole dish, transfer to the oven, and cook for about 2 hours, basting the meat regularly.

Cut the eggplants in half lengthwise, then cut across into slices 3/4 inch thick. Heat the olive oil in a large frying pan, toss the eggplant with the garlic and ground cumin, and fry in the hot oil for 2 minutes, until sealed and golden on both sides. Remove the lid from the lamb, tuck in the eggplant, then cover again and bake for another 30 minutes. The lamb should be very tender, with little sauce remaining.

Serve with Israeli couscous, either plain or flavored with saffron.

HOT TIP If you prefer, you can replace the spiced eggplant with root vegetables such as turnips, parsnips, and carrots. Lightly seal them in the pan after frying the onion and then braise in the oven with the lamb.

4 x 16–18 oz. lamb shanks
1/4 cup vegetable oil
1 onion, finely chopped
1/2 inch piece of fresh ginger root, finely chopped
1 teaspoon ground cinnamon
14 ounce can of tomatoes, chopped
2/3 cup fresh orange juice
1 1/4 cups meat stock or water
Salt and freshly ground black pepper

For the tchermila paste:
1 teaspoon saffron strands
3 garlic cloves, crushed
1 teaspoon coriander seeds
1 teaspoon cumin seeds
1 serrano chile, seeded
1 onion, finely grated
1 tablespoon Harissa, (see p.156)
1 teaspoon hot paprika
1/4 cup olive oil

For the spiced eggplant:
2 large eggplants
1/2 cup olive oil
2 garlic cloves, crushed
1 teaspoon ground cumin

Asian-style steak au poivre

This take on the classic French peppered steak is inspired by my love of oriental food. The vegetables should remain crisp, the steak peppery, with a slightly sweet sauce.

Mix the cracked peppercorns together and then, using the heel of your hand, press them evenly over one side of each steak. Leave for 30 minutes.
Heat the oil in a large, heavy frying pan until smoking. Season the steaks with salt, then add them to the pan, pepper-side down. Fry over medium heat, turning once, for 3–4 minutes for medium-rare, longer if you prefer your meat more cooked. Remove from the pan and keep warm.
Spoon off any fat from the pan, then return the pan to the heat, add the cognac, and flambé it with a match, standing well back. When the flames have died down, add the mirin, corn syrup or honey, ginger, chicken stock, and soy sauces. Bring to a boil, then reduce the heat and simmer until the liquid is reduced by half its volume. Stir in the arrowroot mixture and boil for 1 minute, until thickened, then strain through a fine mesh strainer into a clean pan. Finally whisk in the butter a piece at a time. Keep warm while you prepare the vegetables.
For the vegetables, heat the sesame oil in a wok or large frying pan, add the garlic and ginger, and let infuse for 10 seconds. Add the vegetables, stir-fry for 3–4 minutes, then season. Arrange on 4 serving plates, place the fillet steak on top and pour the sauce over it.

HOT TIP This recipe is also very good made with a meaty fish such as monkfish (angler fish) or turbot.

1 tablespoon black peppercorns, coarsely cracked (see Hot Tip on p.28)
1 tablespoon Szechuan peppercorns, cracked (see Hot Tip on p.28)
4 x 6 ounce fillet steaks
1/4 cup vegetable oil
2 tablespoons cognac
1/4 cup mirin (Japanese sweet rice wine)
1 tablespoon corn syrup or honey
1 inch piece of fresh ginger root, grated
2½ cups well-flavored chicken stock
1/4 cup light soy sauce
1 tablespoon ketjap manis (Indonesian soy sauce)
2 teaspoons arrowroot, mixed with 2 teaspoons cold water
2 tablespoons sweet butter, diced
Salt
For the vegetables:
3 tablespoons sesame oil
1 garlic clove, crushed
1/2 inch piece of fresh ginger root, thinly shredded
4 small pak choi, separated into leaves
1 carrot, sliced
8 scallions, cut in half
4 ounces shiitake mushrooms, thickly sliced
2 red radishes, sliced
1 cup bean sprouts

Seared calf's liver
with chorizo lentils and purple mash

Spicy sausage and lentils are a perfect marriage and I often combine them in a soup. Here they make a hearty accompaniment for seared calf's liver. This dish featured on the menu at the Lanesborough for a while and was very popular.

Pick over the lentils and wash them 3 times in clean water. Put them in a pot, cover with cold water, then bring to a boil and simmer for 30–40 minutes, until tender. Stir from time to time and add more water if the lentils become too dry. When they are cooked they should be moist but not soupy in consistency.

Heat 1 tablespoon of the oil in a frying pan, add the onion, carrot, chile, and spices, and cook for 1 minute. Add the chorizo slices, toss together and cook for a further minute, then add to the lentils. Stir in the coriander and butter, adjust the seasoning, and keep warm.

Preheat the oven to 375°F. Place the whole garlic cloves in a small baking pan, pour the olive oil over them and roast for 10–15 minutes, until tender. Remove from the oven and keep warm.

Meanwhile, cook the whole potatoes in a pan of boiling salted water until tender, then drain and peel (peeling them after cooking preserves their wonderful color). Mash to a smooth purée, return to the heat and stir in the oil, butter, and cream. Season to taste. The purée should be really smooth and silky in texture.

Heat the remaining oil in a frying pan until very hot. Season the liver with salt and pepper and cook for 1 minute on each side, keeping it pink inside.

To serve, put a bed of the spiced lentils on individual serving plates and top with 2 slices of liver. Garnish with the roasted garlic cloves and put a mound of purple mash on the side.

3/4 cup Puy lentils

3 tablespoons vegetable oil

1 onion, chopped

1 carrot, finely diced

1 red chile, seeded and finely diced

1/2 teaspoon ground cumin

1/2 teaspoon ground coriander

5 ounces chorizo sausage, sliced into rounds 1/2 inch thick

1 tablespoon chopped cilantro

2 tablespoons butter

12 garlic cloves

2 tablespoons olive oil

8 x 3 ounce thick slices of calf's liver

Salt and freshly ground black pepper

For the purple mash:

1 lb. truffle potatoes (sometimes labeled as purple or black potatoes)

2 tablespoons olive oil

3/4 stick (1/3 cup) sweet butter

1/2 cup heavy cream

Venison chili
with dried fruit, oregano, and crumbled goat cheese

If you can get hold of Mexican oregano for this chili, do use it. It has a more pungent flavor and grassy aroma than the European variety.

Preheat the oven to 350°. Remove the stems and seeds from the chipotle chiles and roast the chiles in the oven for 1–2 minutes. Place them in a pan, cover with water, then bring to a boil and simmer for 30 minutes. Drain the chiles and place them in a blender. Blitz with enough of their cooking water to make a paste.

Heat the vegetable oil in a large, heavy, flameproof casserole dish (or other flameproof and ovenproof pan). Season the venison with a little salt and then fry in batches in the hot oil until sealed and golden brown on all sides, transferring to a plate as each batch is done. Add the onion, garlic, bay leaf, coriander, and cumin and cook until the onion is soft and translucent. Return the meat to the pan, then add the chipotle chili paste, chili powder, and tomato paste and cook for 10 minutes to amalgamate the flavors. Pour in the beer and stock, add the brown sugar, and cook for 5 minutes, then mix together well, season with salt and pepper, and bring to a boil. Reduce the heat to a simmer and add the dried fruit and oregano. Cover and transfer to the preheated oven to cook for 11/4 hours, stirring occasionally. Add the cooked beans and cook for a further 20 minutes.

To serve, put the chili in a large soup tureen and sprinkle over it the crumbled goat cheese and the corn tortilla chips, if using.

HOT TIP This dish freezes well. Cook for 11/4 hours, then add the beans and let cool. Place in an airtight container and freeze for up to 1 month. For best results, reheat from frozen.

3 chipotle chiles

1/4 cup vegetable oil

11/2 lb. venison (shoulder or leg),
   cut into 3/4 inch dice

1 onion, chopped

2 garlic cloves, crushed

1 bay leaf

1 teaspoon ground coriander

1/2 teaspoon ground cumin

1 tablespoon chili powder

2 tablespoons tomato paste

2/3 cup brown ale or other
   strong-flavored beer

1 quart meat stock

2 tablespoons brown sugar

1/3 cup no-need-to-soak dried
   apricots, cut in half

1/2 cup no-need-to-soak dried prunes,
   cut in half

1 tablespoon dried oregano, preferably
   Mexican

1 cup cooked black beans
   (or kidney beans)

5 ounces strong goat cheese,
   crumbled (about 11/4 cups)

Corn tortilla chips, for garnishing
   (optional)

Salt and freshly ground black pepper

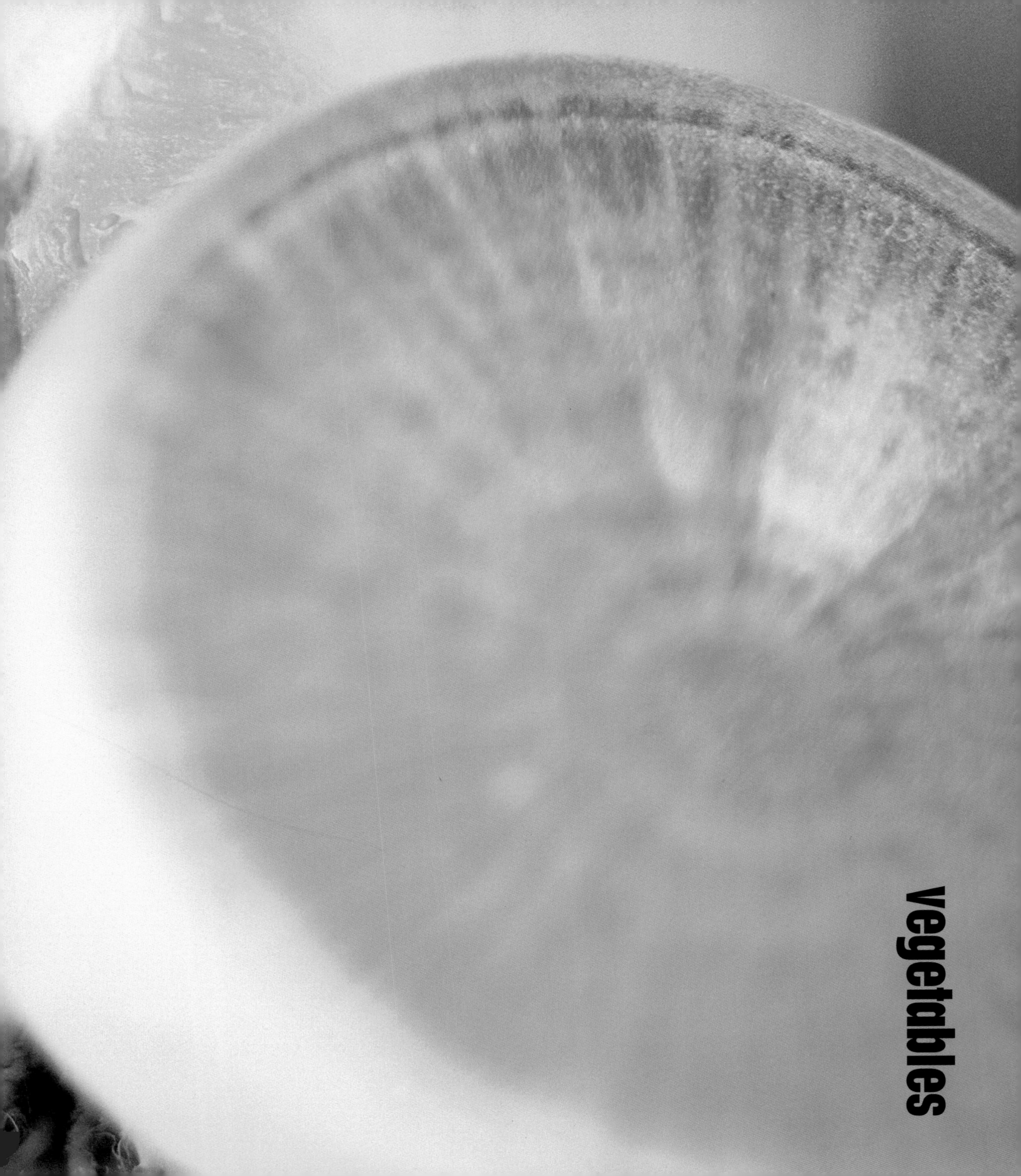

vegetables

Sweet and sour baby onions
with chile and raisin jam

This makes a great accompaniment to grilled chicken or pork. Serve as a relish or as a vegetable side dish, in which case you may want to double the quantities.

Preheat the oven to 400°F. Place the onions in a small roasting pan in a single layer and pour the oil over them. Toss, season lightly, and place in the oven to roast for 12–15 minutes.

Remove from the oven, add the vinegar, stock, and chile jam and stir to combine. Return to the oven for 10 minutes. Place in a serving dish and coat with any remaining cooking juices.

12 ounces baby button onions (or pearl
*   onions), peeled*
1/4 cup vegetable oil
2 tablespoons balsamic vinegar
2/3 cup chicken stock
2 tablespoons Chile and raisin jam
*   (see p.148)*
Salt and freshly ground black pepper

Chargrilled baby eggplants
with ginger pesto

Pesto is such a versatile ingredient that it has become a kitchen basic in recent years. Eggplant and ginger were made for each other, so here's an oriental variation on a theme.

To make the pesto, blend all the ingredients together in a blender or food processor, adding enough oil to form a paste.

Cut the eggplants in half lengthwise, brush with half the olive oil, and place under a hot broiler, cut-side down, for 4–5 minutes or until the skins blister and become slightly charred. Turn the eggplants over, brush with the remaining oil, and broil for 5 minutes, until soft and tender. Serve topped with a dollop of ginger pesto.

8 baby eggplants, 3–4 inches long

6 tablespoons olive oil

For the ginger pesto:

2 tablespoons basil leaves

2 tablespoons mint leaves

2 garlic cloves, crushed

2 tablespoons roasted peanuts

2 inch piece of fresh ginger root, finely chopped

A pinch of sugar

About 2 tablespoons vegetable oil

Salt

Stuffed cherry chile peppers
with olives and Gruyère

Preheat the oven to 400°F. Slice the top off the peppers and remove the seeds. Melt half the butter in a frying pan, add the onion and garlic, and cook for 5 minutes, until softened. Remove from the heat and stir in the pine nuts, olives, herbs, mustard, breadcrumbs, and two-thirds of the cheese. Divide the stuffing between the chile peppers and place them in a baking dish.

Heat the remaining butter in a small pan, stir in the flour, and cook gently for 1–2 minutes. Gradually stir in the milk, then bring to a boil and simmer for a few minutes, until the sauce thickens. Season to taste and stir in the remaining cheese. Pour the sauce over the peppers, cover with foil, and bake for 10–15 minutes. Remove the foil and cook for 10–15 minutes longer, until the topping is golden, then serve immediately.

HOT TIP If you cannot find Hungarian cherry chile peppers they can be replaced with small poblano chiles or even baby red peppers.

6 small to medium Hungarian cherry chile peppers

1/2 stick (1/4 cup) sweet butter

1 red onion, finely chopped

2 garlic cloves, crushed

1/2 cup pine nuts, toasted

3/4 cup black olives, chopped

3 tablespoons chopped mixed herbs (such as basil, oregano, and rosemary)

2 teaspoons Dijon mustard

21/2 cups fresh white breadcrumbs

5 ounces Gruyère cheese (or Swiss cheese), finely grated (about 11/4 cups)

1/4 cup all purpose flour

11/4 cups whole milk

Salt and freshly ground black pepper

Szechuan hot fried vegetables
with spicy bean sauce

You could try other combinations of vegetables here, as long as you choose contrasting colors and textures. The heat comes from Chinese black bean sauce – an easy way of spicing up stir-fries and other oriental dishes.

Heat the oil in a wok or a large frying pan, add the garlic and ginger and let infuse for 30 seconds. Add the vegetables and water chestnuts, and stir-fry for about 3–4 minutes, until crisp and tender. Add the *ketjap manis* and cornstarch paste and stir-fry until the vegetables are glazed in the soy sauce. Add the black bean sauce and 2/3 cup of water and bring to a boil, then season to taste. Transfer to a serving bowl, scatter on the cashews, and serve.

3 tablespoons sesame oil

1 garlic clove, crushed

1 inch piece of fresh ginger root, finely chopped

2 Japanese eggplants, sliced

1 carrot, sliced

1 green and 1 red pepper, cut into 1/2 inch dice

4 ounces sugarsnap peas (a large handful)

8 ounces choi sum (Chinese flowering cabbage), trimmed

12 fresh or canned water chestnuts (peeled if fresh), sliced

1 tablespoon ketjap manis *(Indonesian soy sauce)*

1 teaspoon cornstarch, blended with 2 teaspoons cold water

1/2 cup black bean sauce

3/4 cup cashews

Salt and freshly ground black pepper

Stir-fried Asian greens

In a small bowl combine the soy sauce, black vinegar, sugar, rice wine, cornstarch, and a pinch of salt. Set aside.

Heat a wok or large frying pan over high heat until very hot, add the vegetable oil, then add all the greens and stir-fry for 2 minutes. Transfer to a plate and set aside.

Reheat the wok until very hot, then add the sesame oil. Add the dried chile and peppercorns and cook for 30 seconds, until fragrant. Add the ginger and stir-fry for 10 seconds, then return the greens to the pan and toss well. Add the soy sauce mixture and cook for 1 minute, until the sauce has thickened. Serve immediately.

HOT TIP You should be able to find black vinegar in Chinese grocery stores. It is very dark, with a rich but mild flavor, and is used in many oriental dishes, particularly braises. If necessary, substitute white wine vinegar, or even a splash of balsamic vinegar.

1 tablespoon soy sauce

1 tablespoon Chinese black vinegar (see Hot Tip)

1/2 teaspoon sugar

1 tablespoon rice wine

1 teaspoon cornstarch

1 tablespoon vegetable oil

8 ounces choi sum (Chinese flowering cabbage), cut into pieces

8 ounces pak choi, cut into pieces

8 ounces Chinese cabbage, shredded (about 4 cups)

1 tablespoon sesame oil

1/2 teaspoon finely chopped dried ancho chile

6 Szechuan peppercorns, cracked (see Hot Tip on p.28)

1 1/2 teaspoons finely grated fresh ginger root

Salt

Roasted chile beans

Preheat the oven to 425°F. Blanch the green beans in boiling salted water for 30 seconds, then drain and refresh in cold water. Drain again and dry.

Heat the oils in a flameproof and ovenproof dish or pan, add the garlic and chile and leave over a low heat for a few minutes to infuse. Toss the green beans in the oil, then add the soy sauce and sugar, and toss again so the beans are well coated. Transfer to the oven and roast for 12–15 minutes, until the top is lightly browned. Place in a serving dish and serve immediately.

8 ounces young green beans, trimmed (about 2 cups)

1 tablespoon vegetable oil

1/2 teaspoon sesame oil

2 garlic cloves, crushed

1 green jalapeño chile, seeded and finely sliced

1 tablespoon light soy sauce

1 teaspoon sugar

Horseradish and watercress mash

Cook the potatoes in boiling salted water until very tender, then drain well. Push them through a mesh strainer to give a smooth purée, then return to a gentle heat. Add the milk and cream and beat in the butter. Mix in the horseradish and watercress, season with salt and pepper, and serve.

HOT TIP This mash is also very good with 3/4 cup mild, fresh goat cheese beaten into it.

11/4 lbs. baking potatoes (such as Russet), peeled and cut into chunks
1/2 cup whole milk
1/2 cup heavy cream
3/4 stick (1/3 cup) sweet butter
1 tablespoon finely grated horse-radish root
1 bunch of watercress, stalks removed, leaves roughly chopped
Salt and freshly ground black pepper

Gratin of white roots
with horseradish

Preheat the oven to 350°F. Grease a 10-inch gratin dish with the butter. Cook the parsnips and turnips separately in boiling salted water for 3–4 minutes, then drain well. Season with salt, pepper, and nutmeg, and place in the gratin dish.

Put the cream, milk, and garlic in a pan and bring to a boil. Add the horseradish, then remove from the heat and let infuse for 2–3 minutes. Strain the cream mixture over the parsnips and turnips, making sure the liquid covers them. Bake for 30–40 minutes, until the vegetables are tender and the top golden.

1 tablespoon sweet butter
14 ounces young parsnips, peeled and cut into large pieces (about 31/2-4 cups)
10 ounces young turnips, peeled but left whole
Grated nutmeg
1 pint heavy cream
12/3 cups whole milk
1 garlic clove, crushed
3/4 teaspoon finely grated horse-radish root
Salt and freshly ground black pepper

Aztec corn

This recipe comes from central Mexico, where the Aztecs were the first people to cultivate corn, many centuries ago. There the corn is white, red, or even blue in color. Our more familiar yellow variety will do very well instead, although it is sweeter and less starchy.

When the barbecue is lit on a hot summer's day you must include this delicious and unusual dish of barbecued corn with a heady sauce of cilantro, smoky chiles, lime juice, polenta, and cream.

Preheat the broiler. Broil the chiles about 3–4 inches away from the heat, turning them regularly, until charred all over. Place them in a plastic bag and tie it up. Leave until the chiles are cool enough to handle, then peel, seed, and chop them roughly.
Melt 2 tablespoons of butter and brush onto the corn cobs. Place them under the broiler – or, better still, on a barbecue – and cook, turning occasionally, for 15–20 minutes, until tender and lightly char-grilled.
Heat the remaining butter in a pan, add the scallions, and cook until softened. Stir in the cilantro, chiles, lime juice, polenta, and cream, and simmer for 4–5 minutes or until thickened. Add the tomatoes and finally the corn. Season with salt and pepper and serve hot.

3 green poblano chiles
1/2 stick (1/4 cup) sweet butter
4 ears of corn, husks removed
4 scallions, shredded
2 tablespoons chopped cilantro
1 tablespoon lime juice
1 tablespoon polenta (or cornmeal)
2/3 cup heavy cream
3 plum tomatoes, skinned, seeded and chopped
Salt and freshly ground black pepper

HOT TIP If you cannot find poblano chiles, you could substitute green jalapeños, but remember that they are hotter.

Masala spinach

Heat the oil in a large pot, add the onion, and fry until golden. Add the tomatoes, garlic, ground spices, and chile, and fry for 5–8 minutes, until the tomatoes have reduced and the oil begins to seep out of the mixture. Add the spinach, stir, and cook over high heat until tender. Serve immediately.

1/4 cup vegetable oil
1 onion, finely chopped
14 ounce can of tomatoes, drained and chopped
1 garlic clove, crushed
1/4 teaspoon ground turmeric
1 teaspoon ground coriander
1 teaspoon ground cumin
1 green jalapeño chile, seeded and finely chopped
21/4 lbs. fresh spinach, well washed

ZTEC CORN

Barbecue french fries

These French fries have a little kick!

Cut the potatoes into fries approximately 3 x 1/2 inch. Unless you are going to cook them immediately, place in a bowl of cold water until ready to use.

Drain the potatoes in a colander and then dry in a clean cloth. Heat some vegetable oil in a deep-fat fryer or a large deep pot to 300°F and fry the french fries in small batches until soft and cooked through but not colored. Drain well.

When you are ready to serve the fries, heat the oil to 375°F and, working in batches again, fry them for about 2–3 minutes, until crisp and golden. Place in a baking pan lined with paper towels to absorb excess oil. Season lightly with salt, then add a good sprinkle of the barbecue spice mix.

2 lbs. large potatoes (preferably Russet), peeled or well scrubbed
Vegetable oil for deep-frying
2 tablespoons Barbecue spice mix (see p.157)
Sea salt (or Kosher salt)

HOT TIP After the first frying, the french fries can be drained and kept for several hours at room temperature before completing the cooking.

Smoky patatas bravas

For a heartier dish, I like to add sausage to this classic Spanish tapas. I prepared it this way at the hotel one day and a Spanish waiter informed me it was better than the original – a real compliment!

Boil or steam the potatoes until tender, then drain well. Heat 1/4 cup of the oil in a large frying pan. Add the potatoes and cook over low to medium heat until golden all over. Remove from the pan and set aside.

Add the remaining oil to the pan along with the butter, then add the onion, garlic, and paprika, and cook over low heat until the onion is tender. Return the potatoes to the pan and toss with the onion mixture. Pour in the vinegar and boil until evaporated. Pour in the stock, reduce the heat, and simmer until all the liquid has gone. Add the tomato sauce and chorizo and toss the whole lot together. Cover the pan and let cook gently for 5–8 minutes. The potatoes should be lightly sauced. Adjust the seasoning, sprinkle with the parsley, and serve.

1lb., 10 oz. waxy new potatoes, cut into large chunks
6 tablespoons virgin olive oil
2 tablespoons sweet butter
1 onion, finely chopped
1 garlic clove, crushed
2 teaspoons Spanish smoked paprika
2 tablespoons white wine vinegar
1/2 cup chicken stock
2/3 cup tomato sauce
3 ounces chorizo, skinned and cut into 1/2 inch dice
2 tablespoons chopped flat-leaf parsley
Salt and freshly ground black pepper

Bombay potato cake

Coarsely shred the potatoes on a mandoline, or use the coarse side of a grater. Put them in a large bowl, add the turmeric, and season with salt and black pepper.

Heat a small frying pan over high heat, add the mustard seeds, and cook for about 30 seconds, until they pop. Add the oil, then stir in the curry leaves, chiles, garlic, and cumin, and fry for 2–3 minutes. Add to the potatoes and toss the whole lot together until well mixed. Add the cilantro and adjust the seasoning.

Heat the butter in a frying pan, add the potatoes and fry as one big cake. When golden underneath, invert it on to a large plate, slide it back into the pan, and fry the other side until golden. Cut into wedges to serve.

1 lb. potatoes, peeled
1 teaspoon ground turmeric
1 teaspoon mustard seeds
2 tablespoons vegetable oil
2 curry leaves, finely chopped
2 green Thai chiles, finely chopped
1 garlic clove, crushed
1/2 teaspoon ground cumin
3 tablespoons chopped cilantro
3/4 stick (1/3 cup) sweet butter
Salt and freshly ground black pepper

Black pepper, garlic, and parsley potatoes

Preheat the oven to 375°F. Peel the potatoes and slice them thinly, preferably using a mandoline. Liberally grease a large shallow baking dish with some of the butter, then arrange the potato slices, slightly overlapping, in it. Season with salt. Melt the remaining butter with the garlic and spoon some of it over the potatoes. Season all over with the cracked black pepper and then bake for about 45–50 minutes, basting from time to time with more garlic butter. When the potatoes are lightly golden and tender, remove from the oven, sprinkle over them the chopped parsley, and serve .

1 lb. medium-sized potatoes
  (preferably Russet)
1 stick (1/2 cup) sweet butter
2 garlic cloves, crushed
1–2 tablespoons finely cracked black
  pepper (see Hot Tip on p.28)
2 tablespoons chopped flat-leaf parsley
Coarse salt

CHARGRILLED LEEKS

Chargrilled leeks
basted with mustard butter

Beat together the softened butter, mustard, and lemon juice. Cook the leeks on a charcoal grill (or a ridged grill pan) until tender, basting from time to time with the mustard butter.

1/2 stick (1/4 cup) sweet butter, softened

1 tablespoon whole-grain mustard

1 tablespoon lemon juice

20 baby leeks, trimmed

Salt and freshly ground black pepper

Asian grilled ratatouille

I'm very fond of the original ratatouille but I love creating new versions of it, too. I find the vegetables lend themselves to piquant flavors, such as this Asian interpretation.

Mix together all the ingredients for the marinade, pour it over the vegetables, and let marinate for at least 4 hours, preferably overnight.

Heat a barbecue or a ridged grill pan and place the vegetables on it – in batches if necessary. Cook, turning occasionally and basting with the marinade, until the vegetables are lightly charred and tender. Transfer to a large bowl, pour the remaining marinade over the vegetables. Garnish with the cilantro and serve.

HOT TIP Japanese eggplants are long and thin, light mauve in color and with a sweeter flavor than the larger Mediterranean eggplants. There is no need to salt them before use. Look for them in large supermarkets, Asian food stores and specialist grocery stores.

1 Japanese eggplant, cut into slices 1/2 inch thick

2 zucchini, cut into slices 1/2 inch thick

2 small red onions, peeled and cut into slices 1/2 inch thick

1 red, 1 green, and 1 yellow pepper, cut into 1 1/2 inch dice

A handful of cilantro leaves

For the marinade:

1/2 cup rice vinegar

1 tablespoon sesame oil

1/4 cup maple syrup

Juice of 1/2 lime

2 garlic cloves, crushed

2 inch piece of fresh ginger root, finely grated

2 jalapeño chiles, seeded and finely chopped

Artichokes
with chile aïoli

This uses baby artichokes (sometimes called *poivrade*), which are picked before the choke has formed and can be eaten whole. They are very tender, with a delicate flavor, and need hardly any preparation at all.

First prepare the aïoli: put the garlic, chiles, and a little salt in a bowl. Add the egg yolks and lemon juice and beat well. Gradually add the olive oil, drop by drop at first, whisking constantly, until the mixture becomes smooth and thick. Season to taste with salt and pepper, then set aside.

For the artichokes, put the water and salt in a large pot and bring to a boil. Add the oil, then the artichokes, and simmer for about 10 minutes, until the artichokes are tender (they should float to the top). Drain well, place on a serving dish, and serve with the aïoli.

1 quart water
1 teaspoon salt
1/4 cup vegetable oil
11/4 lbs. baby artichokes, trimmed
   and cut in half vertically
For the aïoli:
3 garlic cloves, crushed
2 red serrano chiles, seeded and
   finely chopped
2 egg yolks
1 tablespoon lemon juice
3/4 cup olive oil
Salt and freshly ground black pepper

Chili willies
spicy plantain chips

Plantains are a member of the banana family and are found everywhere in the Caribbean. During my time there, I saw them served in soups, vegetable dishes, and salads, but my favorite way to use them is this simple, strange-sounding recipe, where they are fried and dusted with chili powder. Served warm or cold, they make an ideal accompaniment to pre-dinner drinks.

Peel the plantains under cold running water to avoid staining your hands. Then, preferably using a mandoline, cut them lengthwise into slices about 1/8 inch thick. Place them in a bowl, cover with the chili oil, and let marinate for 1 hour.
Heat some vegetable oil in a deep-fat fryer or a large, deep pot to 350°F. Drop the plantain slices into the oil a few at a time and fry until golden and crisp. Drain on paper towels. When all the chips are done, place them in a bowl, season with salt, and dust lightly with the chili powder. Toss gently.

4 large green plantains
2/3 cup Chili oil (see p.152)
Vegetable oil for deep-frying
1/2 teaspoon chili powder
Salt

HOT TIP Any ground spice mix can be used as an alternative to the chili powder – for example, Colombo, Sri Lankan, or Barbecue spice mix (see pages 156–157).

RTICHOKES WITH CHILE AÏOLI

salads

Slow-roasted tomato salad
with Tunisian hot dressing

Preheat the oven to 225°F. Place the tomatoes in a shallow baking pan, sprinkle over them the roasted cumin and coriander seeds, sea salt, sugar, and oil, and roast slowly in the oven for about 25–30 minutes, until they begin to soften and dry slightly.
Meanwhile, combine all the ingredients for the dressing in a bowl and let stand at room temperature for the flavors to meld.
Put the warm tomatoes in a serving dish, pour the spicy dressing over them and serve, either at room temperature or cold.

12 firm, small to medium plum tomatoes cut in half
1/2 teaspoon each of cumin and coriander seeds, roasted in a dry frying pan
11/2 teaspoons coarse sea salt (or Kosher salt)
2 teaspoons sugar
1/2 cup olive oil
For the dressing:
1 teaspoon Harissa (see p.156)
1/2 garlic clove, crushed
1/2 red onion, finely chopped
2 tablespoons chopped cilantro
Juice and zest of 1 orange
1/4 cup peanut oil

Roasted beet, feta, and apricot salad

I love the combination of salty feta cheese with sweet beet and apricot, pepped up by a little chile. A colorful salad with heavenly flavors.

Preheat the oven to 350°F. Trim the leafy tops off the beets and scrub the bulbs well. Place in a baking pan, drizzle the peanut oil over them, cover the pan with foil, and bake for 1–11/2 hours, until tender. Remove from the oven and let cool, then peel carefully or rub off the skins. Place in a bowl.
Blanch the apricots in boiling water for 1 minute to loosen the skin, plunge into iced water, then peel them. Cut in half, remove the pit, and place the apricots in a bowl.

To make the vinaigrette, mix together the vinegar, honey, and chile, whisk in both the oils and season with salt and pepper.
Dress the beets and the apricots with the vinaigrette (keeping them separate, otherwise the beets will "bleed" into the apricots) and leave for 20 minutes to marinate. Arrange on a serving plate, sprinkle the crumbled feta cheese and the walnuts over them, and serve at room temperature.

2 lbs. baby beets
3 tablespoons peanut oil
1 lb. fresh apricots
4 ounces feta cheese, crumbled (about 1 cup)
2 tablespoons walnuts
For the vinaigrette:
2 teaspoons sherry vinegar
2 teaspoons honey
1 serrano chile, thinly sliced
3 tablespoons olive oil
3 tablespoons peanut oil
Salt and freshly ground black pepper

SLOW-ROASTED TOMATO SALAD

Roasted beet and basil salad
with creamed horseradish dressing

Preheat the oven to 350°F. Trim the beet tops, leaving 3/4 inch of the stalk attached. Wash them well, then wrap them in 2 foil packages, place on a baking sheet and roast for 1–11/2 hours or until tender. Unwrap the beets and leave until cool enough to handle.

Peel them, cut in half, and place in a large bowl.

For the dressing, whisk together the sour cream or crème fraîche, horseradish, vinegar, mustard, lemon zest, and some seasoning. Add the oil in a thin stream, whisking until emulsified.

Pour the dressing over the beets, toss well together, and transfer to a salad bowl. Scatter the basil over them and serve.

24 baby beets

6 tablespoons sour cream or crème fraîche

2 tablespoons grated horseradish root

2 tablespoons cider vinegar

2 teaspoons Dijon mustard

1/2 teaspoon grated lemon zest

6 tablespoons vegetable oil

10 basil leaves, snipped into small piece

Salt and freshly ground black pepper

Hot and bitter salad

A simple, vibrantly-colored addition to any salad repertoire. This is great with grilled or roast chicken.

Whisk all the ingredients for the dressing together until emulsified.

Toss the salad greens in the dressing, adjust the seasoning, if necessary, and serve.

A selection of hot and bitter salad green – choose from arugula, watercress, chicory, radicchio, dandelion, mizuna, and nasturtium

For the dressing:

2 tablespoons sherry vinegar

1 teaspoon Dijon mustard

2 tablespoons walnut oil

6 tablespoons olive oil

A pinch of sugar

Salt and freshly ground black pepper

gado gado

This is a traditional salad from Indonesia, consisting of crunchy vegetables and bean sprouts with a spicy-sweet peanut dressing. Serve as a refreshing light meal or snack.

For the sauce, heat 5 tablespoons of the sesame oil in a small saucepan and fry the chile in it until soft. In another pan, heat the peanut butter, then add the stock or water, mango chutney, and coconut milk, and boil for 2 minutes. Add the chile and its oil and remove from heat, then add the garlic, soy sauce, the remaining sesame oil, and the sugar. Season to taste and add the lemon juice; the sauce may separate slightly. Keep it warm.

Boil the potato until tender, drain, then peel while it is still hot. Slice and keep it warm. Cook the carrots and beans separately in boiling salted water, retaining their crispness. Drain them and add to the potatoes, along with the cucumber and bean sprouts.

To serve, season the warm vegetables. Arrange the Napa cabbage leaves on serving plates and top with the warm vegetables and quail eggs. Coat lightly with the sauce and serve.

HOT TIP This is also very good with the addition of some sliced tofu, fried in a little vegetable oil until golden brown.

1 waxy potato

2 carrots, cut into matchsticks

1/4 lb. young green beans (about 3/4 cup)

1/2 cup cucumber, cut into matchsticks

1 cup bean sprouts

1/2 Napa cabbage, leaves separated

8 quail eggs, hard-boiled, shelled and
cut in half

Salt and freshly ground black pepper

For the peanut sauce:

6 tablespoons sesame oil

1 red Thai chile, seeded and finely
chopped

1/2 cup smooth peanut butter

6 tablespoons vegetable stock or water

2 tablespoons mango chutney

5 tablespoons coconut milk

1 garlic clove, crushed

1 tablespoon soy sauce

2 teaspoons brown sugar

Juice of 1 lemon

Sicilian potato and caper salad
with mustard dressing

Cook the potatoes in boiling salted water until just tender, then drain and leave until cool enough to handle. Slice them into circles about 1/2 inch thick. Then place in a bowl and add the onion, capers, and oregano.

In a separate bowl, whisk together the oil, vinegar, and mustard, and season with salt and pepper. Pour the dressing over the potatoes and toss together. I prefer to serve this salad warm but it can also be eaten cold.

1 lb. waxy new potatoes, scrubbed

1 red onion, finely chopped

1 teaspoon superfine capers, rinsed and
drained

1 teaspoon chopped oregano

1/2 cup extra virgin olive oil

2 tablespoons red wine vinegar

1 teaspoon Dijon mustard

Salt and freshly ground black pepper

Rujak

This refreshing hot, sweet and sour fruit salad is from Bali, where it is a popular snack. It makes a wonderful appetizer or an addition to any buffet. Topped with ice cream, it can also be served as an intriguing dessert.

Put the palm sugar and tamarind in a small pan with 1/2 cup of water and a pinch of salt. Boil for 2 minutes, then add the chiles and let infuse for a few minutes.

Place all the chopped fruit in a serving bowl and pour the hot syrup mixture over them. Mix in gently and well, then let cool to room temperature before serving.

1/4 cup palm sugar (jaggery)

2 tablespoons tamarind paste

3 red Thai chiles, seeded and finely chopped

1 small pineapple, peeled, cored, and cut into small wedges

1 green mango, peeled, pitted, and slice

1 pink grapefruit, peeled and cut into segments

1 green apple, peeled, cored, and cut int 1/2 inch dice

1 papaya, peeled, seeded, and cut into wedges

Salt

spicy seafood salad

Scrub the mussels under cold running water, removing the beards and discarding any open mussels that don't close when tapped on a work surface. Place the mussels in a steamer and steam over high heat until opened. Remove from the steamer and discard the shells.

Heat the oil in a frying pan, add the shrimp and squid, and fry over high heat for 1–2 minutes only. Add the shelled mussels and place in a bowl.

Mix together all the ingredients for the dressing and pour it over the seafood. Let cool and serve at room temperature.

2 1/4 lbs. mussels

2 tablespoons peanut oil

1 lb. large raw shrimp, peeled and de-veined

1 lb. small squid, cut into small sections

For the dressing:

2 garlic cloves, crushed

2 tablespoons finely chopped cilantro

1 inch piece of fresh ginger root, finely chopped

4 kaffir lime leaves, finely shredded

1 1/4 cups unsweetened coconut cream

2 tablespoons Asian sweet chile sauce (see p.147)

Juice and zest of 1 lime

a small handful cilantro leaves

12 small mint leaves

smoked eel, beet, and apple salad
with wasabi crème fraîche

Preheat the oven to 375°F. Wrap the beets in foil, place on a baking tray, and bake for 1–1 1/2 hours, until tender. Remove from the oven and leave until cool enough to handle, then peel, slice, and set aside.

Put the crème fraîche, cream, wasabi paste, lemon juice and zest, apples, onion, and some salt and pepper in a bowl and mix until the cream thickens enough to coat the apple and onion. Place a 3-inch pastry cutter on each of 4 serving plates, then arrange some beet slices neatly on the bottom. Cover with avocado slices, then some eel fillet. Top with horseradish cream, more beets, avocado, and more horseradish cream, and finally the last of the eel fillet. Carefully remove the rings, scatter the cilantro leaves over them, and serve.

4 medium beets

2 tablespoons crème fraîche (or heavy cream)

2/3 cup heavy cream

1/2 teaspoon wasabi paste (Japanese horseradish)

Juice and zest of 1 lemon

2 apples, preferably Granny Smith, peeled, cored, and finely diced

1 red onion, finely diced

1 avocado, peeled, pitted, and cut into slices 1/4 inch thick

8 large smoked eel fillets, sliced in half

2 tablespoons cilantro leaves

Salt and freshly ground black pepper

Smoked salmon and crab sushi salad
with sansho dressing

This Japanese-inspired salad uses wasabi tobiko, which is the orangey-red roe of a type of flying fish. It is available in small plastic tubs from Oriental grocery stores, but just leave it out if you cannot find any.

Place the rice in a saucepan, pour in 11/2 cups of water and quickly bring to a boil. Reduce the heat, cover, and simmer until all the liquid has been absorbed. Remove from the heat and set aside for 5 minutes.

In a small pan, gently heat the vinegar and sugar. Spread the cooked rice out on a large flat tray, then sprinkle over it the vinegar and sugar. Gently mix it with the rice to give a sheen to it and then let cool (traditionally the rice is cooled by fanning it with a cloth).

Mix the crabmeat with the salad greens, radishes, pink ginger, and hijiki, then toss with the cooled sushi rice.

Place 4 lightly oiled ring molds or pastry cutters about 3 inches in diameter on a tray, and line the inner edge with a band of smoked salmon. Fill the center with the sushi salad, taking it right to the top.

Mix together all the ingredients for the dressing.

To serve, place one ring on each serving plate and then carefully remove the ring. Top each with a little wasabi tobiko, if using, and pour a little of the dressing around it.

HOT TIP For me, hijiki is the tastiest of all seaweeds. It is full of iodine and essential minerals and has a pleasant, chewy texture. There is no need to soak it before using. You should be able to find it in Japanese food stores or health food stores.

3/4 cup short grain rice, rinsed
1 tablespoon rice vinegar
2 teaspoons sugar
41/2 ounces fresh crabmeat (1/2 cup)
4 ounces mixed bitter salad greens, such
as peashoots, dandelion,
  mizuna and frisée, torn into small
  pieces (about 2 large handfuls)
4 red radishes, thinly sliced
1 tablespoon pickled pink ginger,
  shredded
1/2 ounce hijiki seaweed
8 ounces thinly sliced smoked salmon
1 tablespoon wasabi tobiko (optional)
For the dressing:
1/2 teaspoon sansho (Japanese pepper)
2 tablespoons red wine vinegar
2 tablespoons light soy sauce
1/4 cup sesame oil
1/4 cup vegetable oil
Juice of 1/2 lemon
2 teaspoons Asian sweet chile sauce
  (see p.147)

seared tuna tartare
and noodle salad

This simple and impressive salad is ideal for summer. Light in flavor and texture, it can be prepared well in advance and put together when needed. Be sure to use very, very fresh tuna, as it is barely cooked.

Cut the tuna fillet into neat 3/4 inch dice and place in a bowl. Add the sweet chile sauce, half the sesame oil, plus the garlic and ginger, then cover and chill for 2 hours.

Mix together all the ingredients for the dressing and set aside.

Place the noodles in a large bowl and pour over them enough boiling water to cover. Leave for 1 minute and then drain in a colander.

Heat the remaining sesame oil in a wok or large frying pan over high heat. Add the tuna and its marinating juices and toss for about 30 seconds to seal. Remove from the pan and set aside. Add all the vegetables to the pan and stir-fry for 1 minute or until just cooked and still crunchy. Return the tuna to the pan along with the vegetables, add the noodles, and toss well. Pour in the dressing and pile on to serving plates. Sprinkle on some black sesame seeds and cilantro leaves and serve immediately.

1 lb. sushi-quality fresh tuna fillet

3 tablespoons Asian sweet chile sauce (see p.147)

1/4 cup sesame oil

1 garlic clove, crushed

1 inch piece of fresh ginger root, cut into fine strips

11 ounces egg thread noodles

1 1/2 cups bean sprouts

1 red pepper, cut into fine strips

1/4 cucumber, seeded and cut into fine strips

1 bunch of choi sum (Chinese flowering cabbage), trimmed

2 ounces (a large handful) mizuna (oriental mustard leaf)

Black sesame seeds and cilantro leaves, for garnishing

For the dressing:

1 teaspoon sugar

2 teaspoons rice vinegar

2 tablespoons nam pla (Thai fish sauce)

2 tablespoons dark soy sauce

Juice of 1 lime

Grilled squid and melon salad
with hot and sour kaffir dressing

What I like about this salad is the combination of chewy fish and tangy, lightly chargrilled fruit. It makes a wonderful appetizer for a summer dinner.

Slit the squid bodies open, cut them into large rectangles, and then score in a diamond pattern on the inner side with a sharp knife (this makes them curl up attractively when cooked). Leave the tentacles in large pieces. Mix all the marinade ingredients together in a large bowl, add the squid and melon, and let marinate at room temperature for 2–3 hours.

Heat the broiler to its highest setting. Remove the squid and melon from the marinade, place on the broiler pan and broil for 4–5 minutes. Transfer to a bowl and sprinkle the herbs over them.

Put all the ingredients for the dressing into a pan and heat gently. Pour the dressing over the squid and melon. Let cool to room temperature before serving.

8 ounces cleaned squid

1/4 honeydew melon, peeled and cut into
  thin wedges

A slice of watermelon, peeled and cut
  into thin wedges

1 tablespoon roughly chopped
  mint leaves

1 tablespoon roughly chopped
  cilantro leaves

For the marinade:

1/2 cup olive oil

1/4 teaspoon chili powder

1 garlic clove

Juice of 1 lime

2 tablespoons sugar

For the dressing:

3 tablespoons nam pla (Thai fish sauce)

2 tablespoons lime juice

1 garlic clove, crushed

1 red and 1 green chile, seeded and
  finely chopped

1 teaspoon brown sugar

4 kaffir lime leaves, finely shredded

Peppered chicken liver salad
with gorgonzola dressing

This salad crosses several different flavor spectrums – tangy, sweet, and slightly hot. The creamy bite of the gorgonzola makes a perfect foil for the chicken livers.

For the dressing, put the cheese and hot water in a bowl and crush it to a smooth purée with a fork. Stir in the vinegar, then add the crème fraîche and lemon juice, and season to taste. Add the chives.

Cook the sugarsnaps and green beans separately in boiling salted water. Drain, refresh under cold running water, and drain again.

Wrap the peppercorns in a lint free towel and place on a work surface. Using a hammer or rolling pin, crack the peppercorns. Place on a plate, add the cleaned chicken livers, and roll them in the pepper.

Season with a little salt.

Heat the oil in a frying pan until nearly smoking. Add half the chicken livers in a single layer and cook for 1 minute on each side, until colored. Transfer to a plate and keep warm while you cook the remaining livers. Place the greens in a large bowl, add all the vegetables except the cherry tomatoes, and toss with the gorgonzola dressing. Pile the salad up on 4 serving plates. Top with the peppered chicken livers and garnish with the cherry tomato halves.

3 ounces (a handful) sugarsnap peas
3 ounces (a handful) young green beans
1 teaspoon black peppercorns
12 ounces fresh chicken livers, cleaned
1/4 cup vegetable oil
4 ounces (2 large handfuls) mixed
  green salad greens
2 medium carrots, cut into fine strips
6 cherry tomatoes, cut in half
Salt and freshly ground black pepper
For the gorgonzola dressing:
2 ounces (1/2 cup) gorgonzola cheese
1/4 cup hot water
1 tablespoon champagne vinegar
1/2 cup crème fraîche (or heavy cream)
Juice of 1/2 lemon
2 tablespoons chopped chives

Creole chicken salad
with black beans, corn, and oregano–hot pepper vinaigrette

Season the chicken breasts with salt and a little pepper and then dust with the spice mix. Fry them in a little hot oil – or chargrill them, which I think is better!

While the chicken is cooking, make the vinaigrette: place the wine vinegar, mustard, and garlic in a bowl, then whisk in the oil a little at a time.

Add the Tabasco, lemon juice, and oregano.

Place the salad greens, cooked beans, corn, and tomatoes in a large bowl, pour in the vinaigrette, and toss well together. Season to taste. Cut the hot chicken into 3/4 inch dice and scatter on top of the salad, then serve immediately – a wonderful blend of hot and cold.

4 x 7 ounce chicken breasts, boned
  and skinned
2 tablespoons Blackened Cajun spice mix
  (see p.157)
Oil for frying (optional)
1 head of chicory, leaves separated
2 romaine lettuces, leaves separated
1 bunch of watercress
1/2 cup black beans, cooked
1/4 cup corn
12 cherry tomatoes, cut in half
Salt and freshly ground black pepper

For the vinaigrette:
2 tablespoons white wine vinegar
2 teaspoons Dijon mustard
1 garlic clove, crushed
1/2 cup olive oil
4 drops of Tabasco sauce
1 teaspoon lemon juice
1 teaspoon chopped oregano

Warm steak salad
with horseradish, mustard, and balsamic juices

For the dressing, place the mustard, horseradish, and garlic in a bowl, add the vinegar, and leave for 10–15 minutes to infuse. Whisk in the oil to form a dressing. Season with salt and pepper and then add the cilantro.

Heat the vegetable oil in a small frying pan until almost smoking. Season the beef with salt and pepper, add to the pan, and fry over medium heat for 8–10 minutes, turning once (otherwise cook in a hot oven for 5–8 minutes); this should give medium-rare to medium meat. Remove from the pan and keep warm.

Return the pan in which the meat was cooked to the heat and add the meat stock. Bring to a boil and boil for 1 minute, stirring and scraping the bottom of the pan to deglaze, then add to the dressing and mix thoroughly.

Place the salad greens and vegetable strips in a bowl and toss with half the dressing. Put the salad in a serving dish. Slice the tenderloin thinly and arrange on top of the salad. Pour on the remaining dressing and serve.

2 tablespoons vegetable oil

1 lb. best-quality beef tenderloin

5 ounce bag of mixed salad greens
(about 3 large handfuls)

1 large carrot, cut into strips 1/8 inch thick

1/2 celeriac, cut into strips 1/8 inch thick

1 large beet, cut into strips
1/8 inch thick

1 red onion, thinly sliced

Salt and freshly ground black pepper

For the dressing:

1 teaspoon Dijon mustard

1 teaspoon grated horseradish root

1 garlic clove, crushed

1/4 cup balsamic vinegar

1/2 cup vegetable oil

1 tablespoon chopped cilantro

1/2 cup meat stock

pasta, rice and

BUCATINI WITH CLAMS, GARLIC AND CHORIZ

Bucatini
with clams, garlic, and chorizo

Scrub the clams under cold running water, discarding any open ones that don't close when tapped on a work surface. Set aside.

Cook the pasta in a large pot of boiling salted water until *al dente*.

Meanwhile, heat half the oil in a large pot over medium heat, add the garlic, and cook for 1 minute without letting it color. Stir in the parsley, then add the clams and pour in the white wine. Cover with a lid and let steam for 2 minutes. Add the tomatoes, chile, and chorizo, and pour in the remaining olive oil. Cover again and let cook for a further 2 minutes, until the clams open.

Drain the pasta. Stir the clam and chorizo sauce, then toss with the pasta and serve immediately into individual bowls.

HOT TIP The bucatini could be replaced by another long pasta, such as spaghetti or fettuccine. For a real treat, you could also add some more shellfish to the sauce – mussels and cockles would be good.

48 baby venus clams

1 lb. bucatini pasta

6 tablespoons olive oil

2 garlic cloves, crushed

1 tablespoon finely chopped flat-leaf parsley

5 tablespoons dry white wine

14 ounce can of tomatoes, chopped

1/2 teaspoon finely chopped dried peperoncino chile

3 ounces chorizo, outer casing removed, cut into 1/4 inch dice

Fried ginger noodles
with pak choi and scallions

Place the noodles in a large bowl and pour enough boiling water over them to cover. Leave for 30 seconds, then drain in a colander.

Heat the vegetable oil in a wok or a large frying pan, add the ginger and garlic, then add the pak choi leaves and stir-fry for 1 minute. Add the drained noodles, oyster sauce, soy and fish sauce, and mix well together.

Serve immediately, sprinkled with the shredded scallions.

1 lb. egg thread noodles

2 tablespoons vegetable oil

1 inch piece of fresh ginger root, finely chopped

1 garlic clove, crushed

4 pak choi, separated into leaves

2 tablespoons oyster sauce

1 tablespoon dark soy sauce

1 teaspoon nam pla (Thai fish sauce)

4 scallions, finely shredded

Wok-fried noodles
with dry-spiced beef

Bring 2 quarts of water to a boil, add the beef, and poach for 1 hour or until it is so tender that the meat fibers separate easily. Let cool a little, and then shred it finely with a fork.

Put the garlic, palm sugar, chiles, galangal, shrimp paste, and ground cloves in a blender or food processor and blitz to a coarse paste. Heat the oil in a frying pan and cook the paste over medium heat for 2–3 minutes, until fragrant. Add the finely shredded beef, mix well, and sauté until the moisture from the spice paste has evaporated and the meat is tacky. Season to taste.

Place the noodles in a bowl, pour plenty of boiling salted water over them, and leave for 30 seconds to swell. Drain them well, toss with the spiced beef, and serve immediately.

12 ounces beef skirt

1 tablespoon crushed garlic

1 tablespoon palm sugar

2 red Thai chiles, seeded and finely chopped

1 inch piece of fresh galangal (or ginger root), peeled and finely sliced

2 teaspoons blachan *(dried shrimp paste)*

1/2 teaspoon ground cloves

2 tablespoons vegetable oil

1 lb. egg thread noodles

Salt and freshly ground black pepper

Steamed Napa cabbage wraps

A type of Asian dolmades, this makes a wonderful side dish or starter. Vegetarians could replace the fish sauce with light soy sauce.

Heat the oil in a pan, add the diced eggplant and fry over medium heat until golden and tender. Lower the heat, add the onion, garlic, and lemongrass and cook for 3–4 minutes, until the onion is softened. Transfer to a bowl, add the cooked rice, tomatoes, and herbs, then season with the fish sauce and sweet chile sauce. Let marinate for at least 4 hours, preferably overnight.

Using a sharp knife, carefully remove at least a third of the stem from each Napa cabbage leaf.

Blanch the leaves in boiling salted water for 30 seconds, then transfer to a bowl of iced water using a slotted spoon. Put the leaves on a cloth to drain and then lay them out on a board.

Place 2 good heaped tablespoons of the filling at the base of each leaf and roll up, folding in the sides. To serve, reheat in a steamer or place in an ovenproof dish with about 1/2 cup water, cover with foil, and warm through in the oven. Serve with a little warm sweet chile sauce.

HOT TIP Add some cooked shrimp or lobster to the filling.

1/2 cup vegetable oil

1 eggplant, finely diced

1 onion, finely chopped

1 garlic clove, crushed

1 tablespoon finely chopped lemongrass

1 cup cooked sushi or basmati rice

6 medium tomatoes, skinned, seeded and diced

1/2 tablespoon roughly chopped mint

1 tablespoon roughly chopped cilantro

1 tablespoon roughly chopped basil

3 tablespoons nam pla *(Thai fish sauce)*

6 tablespoons Asian sweet chile sauce (see p.147), plus extra for serving

8 large outer leaves of Napa cabbage

Bigoli
with spicy meat sauce

Bigoli is a thick whole wheat spaghetti from Venice, usually served with robust sauces such as anchovy and onion, or this spicy mixture of ground pork and chicken livers. If you can't find bigoli, bucatini makes a good substitute.

Season the pork with salt and pepper. Heat 1/4 cup of the oil in a heavy frying pan, then add the pork and cook over high heat until sealed all over. Stir in the vegetables, garlic, and chili flakes, and cook for 2–3 minutes. Add the diced chicken livers, cover the pan, and cook for 5 minutes, then pour in the red wine, cover again, and cook for 2 minutes longer. Stir in the tomato paste, sauce, sugar, and a little salt, then reduce the heat, cover, and cook for about 20–30 minutes, stirring occasionally.

Cook the pasta in plenty of boiling salted water until *al dente*, then drain well. Toss the pasta with the remaining oil and some nutmeg, salt, and pepper. Add the meat sauce and chopped sage, toss together, then serve.

HOT TIP It's a myth that you need to add oil to the cooking water to prevent pasta sticking. Just cook the pasta in plenty of boiling water until *al dente* and it will be fine. Once it has been drained, toss it in a little oil to help keep the strands separate.

12 ounces ground pork
1/4 cup, plus 2 tablespoons olive oil
1 onion, finely chopped
1 carrot, finely chopped
1 celery stalk, finely chopped
1 garlic clove, finely chopped
1 teaspoon dried red chili flakes
4 ounces chicken livers, cleaned and finely diced
2/3 cup red wine
2 tablespoons tomato paste
2/3 cup tomato sauce
A pinch of sugar
1 lb. bigoli pasta
Grated nutmeg
1 tablespoon chopped sage
Salt and freshly ground black pepper

Mushroom pad thai

Pad Thai is one of many noodle stir-fries prepared throughout the Far East. I first experienced it during a trip to Thailand, where it is practically a national dish. It is usually made with dried rice vermicelli but any oriental noodle is fine – even an Italian pasta such as linguine would do in a pinch.

Soak the noodles in plently of cold water for 10 minutes, then drain. Cook in a large pot of boiling salted water for 5 minutes, then drain, refresh under cold running water, and drain again thoroughly.

Heat half the oil in a wok or a large frying pan, add the garlic, chiles, and shiitake mushrooms, and fry for 2–3 minutes, until the mushrooms are browned all over. Add the noodles and toss with the mushrooms, then add the fish sauce and soy sauce and mix well. Remove the mixture from the wok and keep warm.

Wipe out the wok and heat the remaining oil in it. Add the beaten eggs and cook until lightly scrambled. Return the noodles to the pan, mix well, and season with salt and pepper to taste. Turn out on to a serving dish and sprinkle with the scallions, cilantro leaves, and peanuts.

1 lb. rice noodles
2 tablespoons vegetable or peanut oil
3 garlic cloves, crushed
2 serrano chiles, thinly sliced
10 ounces shiitake mushrooms, thickly sliced
1 tablespoon nam pla (Thai fish sauce)
2 tablespoons ketjap manis (Indonesian soy sauce)
2 eggs, beaten
4 scallions, thinly shredded
2 tablespoons cilantro leaves
1/4 cup roasted peanuts, chopped
Salt and freshly ground black pepper

Shiitake and butternut squash orzotto
with chile pecorino

Orzo is a rice-shaped pasta, which I have used here instead of rice to make a sort of risotto – or orzotto. Coincidentally, after devizing this recipe, I discovered that you could buy pecorino (Romano) cheese with chile in it. If you manage to find some, cut it into fine shavings and substitute it for the grated pecorino. Either cut down the amount of jalapeño or leave it out entirely, depending on your chile tolerance – the chile pecorino is surprisingly strong.

Heat the olive oil in a heavy pan, add the garlic and scallions and cook for 1 minute. Add the orzo and cook for a further minute, stirring to coat the pasta with the oil and garlic. Stir in the squash and cook for 5 minutes. Meanwhile, bring the stock to a boil in a separate pot and keep at simmering point.

Add the stock to the orzo a little at a time, stirring occasionally and making sure the pasta is always just covered by the liquid. After 10 minutes, add the shiitake, then continue adding the stock until the orzo is *al dente*. Remove the pan from the heat, stir in the butter, and season with salt and black pepper to taste.

Mix together the cheese, chile, and mint, scatter them on top of the pasta, and serve immediately.

2 tablespoons virgin olive oil

1 garlic clove, crushed

4 scallions, shredded on the diagonal

1 lb. orzo pasta

1 small butternut squash, peeled, seeded, and cut into 1/2 inch cubes

1 quart well-flavored chicken or vegetable stock

12 shiitake mushrooms, thickly sliced

1 tablespoon sweet butter

2 tablespoons grated pecorino (Romano) cheese

1 jalapeño chile, seeded and finely chopped

1 tablespoon chopped mint

Salt and freshly ground black pepper

Paprika pasta paella

This is based on *fideua*, a classic paella from Valencia made with noodles instead of rice. Here I've used lumachine ("little snails") pasta.

Put the stock and saffron in a pot and bring to a boil, then remove from the heat and set aside.
Heat the oil in a separate pan, add the onion, chili flakes, and garlic, and fry over medium heat for 5 minutes, until golden. Stir in the paprika. Add the eggplant, red pepper, and artichokes, and stir to coat with the paprika, then add the tomatoes.

Lower the heat and cook for 5–8 minutes. Add the hot stock and bring to a boil, then add the pasta and spread it out evenly. Season with salt and pepper, reduce the heat, and cook for 12–15 minutes. Taste the noodles to check they are cooked, then remove from the heat and let rest for a few minutes before serving.

1 quart vegetable or chicken stock
1/2 teaspoon saffron strands
1/4 cup olive oil
1 onion, finely chopped
1 teaspoon dried red chili flakes
1 garlic clove, crushed
1 tablespoon hot Hungarian paprika
1 eggplant, cut into 1/2 inch dice
1 red pepper, cut into 1/2 inch dice
2 prepared artichoke hearts
14 ounce can of chopped tomatoes
1 lb. lumachine pasta
a handful of young green beans, cooked
Salt and freshly ground black pepper

Hot pepper peanut rice

I love the warm, ocher color of this spicy rice, which makes a good accompaniment to just about any grilled meat or fish.

Heat the chili oil and butter in a pan, add the garlic, onion, carrot, celery, and red pepper, and cook over medium heat for 2 minutes. Add the dried chili flakes and rice, and cook for 2–3 minutes, until the rice takes on a red, shiny glaze. Add the chicken stock or water and bring to a boil, stirring occasionally, then add the bay leaf. Reduce the heat, cover the pan, and cook for 12–15 minutes or until the rice is tender and has absorbed the liquid. Stir in the peanuts, adjust the seasoning, and serve.

2 tablespoons Chili oil (see p.152)
2 tablespoons sweet butter
2 garlic cloves, crushed
1/2 onion, finely diced
1 carrot, finely diced
1 celery stalk, finely diced
1 red pepper, finely diced
1 teaspoon dried red chili flakes
11/3 cups long grain rice
2 cups chicken stock or water
1 bay leaf
a heaped 1/2 cup unsalted peanuts
Salt and freshly ground black pepper

enne arrabbiatta

ngry pasta" is a classic Italian dish that uses a little dried chile to spice up a simple tomato sauce. Parmesan vers may wish to top it with a little Parmesan, although this is not traditional. I find it robs the dish of heady power.

make the sauce, heat the oil in a pan, add the li flakes and garlic, and cook over low heat for 1 nute. Add the tomato sauce and bring to a boil, en reduce the heat and simmer until reduced half.

Cook the pasta in plenty of boiling salted water until *al dente*. Drain well and toss with the butter, then season with salt and pepper. Toss the sauce with the pasta and serve right away.

2 tablespoons olive oil
1 teaspoon dried red chili flakes
   (or hot chili paste)
4 garlic cloves, crushed
1 cup tomato sauce
1 lb. penne
2 tablespoons sweet butter
Salt and freshly ground black pepper

renette frittata
ith pepperoni and venus clams

rub the clams under cold running water, discard- g any open ones that don't close when tapped on vork surface. Put them in a large pot, pour in the ite wine, then cover and place on high heat for 2 minutes, until the clams open. Drain in a colan- r, then strain the juices through a fine mesh ainer and put to one side. Shell the clams and t aside.

at 3 tablespoons of the olive oil in a small frying n, add the garlic, and cook over low heat until ftened. Add the red pepper, dried chili flakes, d pepperoni slices, and cook until the pepper is ftened. Then add the clams and their juice and ok for 1 minute. Remove the pan from the heat d set aside.

Cook the pasta in plenty of boiling salted water until *al dente*, then drain well. In a bowl, toss the pasta with the clam and pepper mixture and let cool.

Add the beaten eggs and the parsley to the cooled pasta mixture and season with salt and pepper. In a small frying pan or omelette pan (preferably non-stick), heat the remaining oil. Add the pasta mixture and spread it out with a fork. Reduce the heat and, stirring carefully from time to time, cook until browned underneath and just set. Place a large plate over the pan and invert the frittata on to it. Slide the frittata, browned-side up, back into the pan and cook on the other side for 2 minutes. Turn out on to a serving plate and let cool slightly before cutting into wedges to serve.

30 small venus clams
1/2 cup dry white wine
6 tablespoons olive oil
3 garlic cloves, crushed
1 red pepper, cut into 1/4 inch dice
1/2 teaspoon dried red chili flakes
3 ounces pepperoni, cut into slices
   1 inch thick
9 ounces trenette (linguine)
5 large eggs, lightly beaten
1 tablespoon chopped flat-leaf parsley
Salt and freshly ground black pepper

T TIP If you are not feeling brave enough to turn the frittata over to cook the other side, simply put the n under a hot broiler until the mixture is just set and lightly colored.

SAFFRON AND MUSTARD SEED RI

saffron and mustard seed rice

Put the water, salt, lemon juice and zest, and saffron in a pan and bring to a boil, then let infuse for 5 minutes over very low heat.

Heat the ghee or vegetable oil in another pan, large enough to take the rice, add the mustard seeds, and sauté until they pop and become aromatic. Add the rice and stir to mix with the seeds.

Cook for 1 minute, then add the saffron-infused water. Bring to a boil, reduce the heat, and cover with a tight-fitting lid. Cook gently for about 15 minutes, until the rice is tender and fluffy.

Remove from the heat and leave, covered, for 5 minutes to let the rice steam. Transfer to a serving dish and drizzle the Indian chili oil over it.

21/2 cups water

1/2 teaspoon salt

Juice and zest of 1/2 lemon

1 teaspoon saffron strands

2 tablespoons ghee or vegetable oil

2 teaspoons black mustard seeds

11/2 cups basmati rice, well washed
and drained

2 tablespoons Indian chili oil
(see p.152)

hoppin' John

In America's Deep South, this dish of rice and black-eyed peas is eaten at New Year to bring good luck. If you cannot find black-eyed peas, substitute another type of bean such as kidney or cannellini, but don't expect such good luck if you do!

Although it's not traditional, I find cooking the rice separately from the peas keeps the dish better defined. When they are cooked together, the rice loses its texture.

Heat the oil in a pan, add the bacon, and fry for 5 minutes, until lightly colored. Add the onion, garlic, celery, red pepper, and paprika, and cook for 3 minutes. Add the soaked black-eyed peas and cover with the stock. Bring to a boil, then reduce the heat and cook for about 30 minutes or until the peas are tender.

Meanwhile, cook the rice in plenty of boiling salted water, then drain well. Stir the black-eyed pea mixture into the rice, add the scallions and hot pepper sauce, and season to taste. Sprinkle the cheese on top, if using, and serve right away.

2 tablespoons vegetable oil

9 ounce piece of smoked bacon, cut
into small pieces

1 onion, chopped

2 garlic cloves, crushed

1 celery stalk, chopped

1 red pepper, finely chopped

1 teaspoon smoked paprika

11/2 cups black-eyed peas, soaked
overnight and then drained

1 quart chicken stock

3/4 cup long grain rice

4 scallions, finely shredded

1 teaspoon West Indian hot pepper sauce

3/4 cup grated sharp Cheddar
cheese, (optional)

Salt and freshly ground black pepper

Smoked fish kedgeree
with scrambled eggs

Heat half the butter in a heavy saucepan, add the onion and mushrooms, and cook over low heat for 5–6 minutes, until softened. Stir in the curry paste and cook for 1 minute. Add the cooked rice and stir until well coated in the butter. Add the smoked salmon, cooked smoked haddock, and peas, and season lightly. Keep warm.

In a separate pan, heat the remaining butter and the cream, season with salt and pepper, and then pour in the beaten eggs. Scramble them over a very low heat, keeping them soft and light in texture. Fold the eggs carefully into the rice and transfer to a serving plate. Sprinkle the chopped parsley on top and serve.

1/2 stick (1/4 cup) sweet butter

1 small onion, finely chopped

a scant cup sliced white mushrooms

11/2 teaspoons My curry paste (see p.154

13/4 cups basmati rice, cooked

4 ounces smoked salmon, cut into slivers

12 ounces smoked haddock, cooked and flaked

1/2 cup peas, cooked

6 tablespoons heavy cream

4 eggs, beaten

1 tablespoon chopped parsley

Salt and freshly ground black pepper

Hot and sour yoghurt rice

Wash the rice well, cover with cold water, and let soak for 1 hour. Drain well, then place in a heavy saucepan, add a little salt, and level off the rice. Pour in enough water to cover the rice by 1–2inches. Bring to a boil, cover with a tight-fitting lid, and reduce the heat to low. Leave undisturbed for about 20 minutes, until all the liquid has been absorbed and the rice is tender.

Meanwhile, heat the oil in a frying pan, add the

vegetables, garlic, chiles, cumin, and dried herbs, and cook for 4–5 minutes, until soft. Place in a blender, add the cilantro leaves, lime juice, yoghurt, and 2/3 cup of water, and blitz to a coarse purée. Return to the pan to reheat, then season with salt and pepper.

Fluff up the rice with a fork to separate the grains and release trapped steam. Add the yoghurt spice mix, folding in carefully. Serve hot or cold.

1 lb. basmati rice

2 tablespoons peanut oil

1 celery stalk, chopped

1 onion, chopped

2 green peppers, chopped

4 garlic cloves, crushed

3 jalapeño chiles, seeded and chopped

1 teaspoon ground cumin

1 teaspoon dried thyme

1 teaspoon dried oregano

A good handful of cilantro leaves

Juice of 2 limes

2/3 cup yoghurt

Salt and freshly ground black pepper

SMOKED FISH KEDGEREE

Jalapeño cornbread

Preheat the oven to 375°F. Combine the flour, polenta, salt, baking powder, and sugar in a mixing bowl, and make a well in the center. Add the beaten eggs, melted butter, and milk, and mix well to form a smooth batter. Stir in the chile, corn, and grated cheese. Pour the mixture into a lightly greased 8 inch cake pan or cast-iron frying pan and smooth the surface. Bake for 25 minutes, until golden and firm to the touch. Let cool in the pan a little, then tip out and serve warm, cut into small squares or wedges, with butter.

1 cup plus 2 tablespoons all pupose flour

1 cup fine polenta (cornmeal)

A pinch of salt

4 teaspoons baking powder

1/4 cup sugar

2 eggs, beaten

1 tablespoon melted sweet butter

1 cup whole milk

1 green jalapeño chile, seeded and finely chopped

7 ounce can of corn, drained

2 cups grated Cheddar cheese

Asian-style focaccia

We always serve a variety of breads at the Lanesborough and I invented this one as a means of using my favorite flavorings – cilantro, pickled ginger, and sweet chili. It's been very popular and is surprisingly easy to make.

Sift the flour and salt into a large mixing bowl and stir in the yeast. Mix together 1/4 cup of oil, the water, garlic, ginger, and cilantro, and stir into the flour to form a rough dough. Turn the dough out on to a floured surface and knead until smooth and elastic. Place in a lightly oiled bowl, cover with plastic wrap and let rise at room temperature for 1–11/2 hours, until almost double in size.

Preheat the oven to 400°F. Tip out the dough and knead lightly to knock out the air, then roll out to a square, about 3/4 inch thick. Place in a well-greased 10–12 inch cake pan or on a baking sheet. Using floured fingers, make indentations at 1 inch intervals all over the dough. Drizzle over it the remaining olive oil, then bake for about 25–30 minutes, until golden in color and spongy in texture.

Blend the chili sauce and vegetable oil together and brush it over the surface of the bread two or three times. Serve warm or cold.

11/2 lbs. white bread flour
   (about 6 cups)
1 tablespoon salt
1 envelope of rapid rise yeast
2 cups lukewarm water
1/4 cup, plus 2 tablespoons olive oil
1 garlic clove, crushed
3 tablespoons pickled pink ginger, dried
   in a cloth, roughly chopped
1/4 cup roughly chopped
   cilantro
6 tablespoons Asian sweet chili sauce
   (see p.147)
3 tablespoons vegetable oil

HOT TIP The dough can be used as a pizza base and baked with your favourite toppings.

Mediterranean chile, olive, and cumin fougasse

Sift the flour and salt into a large mixing bowl and stir in the yeast. Mix together the water, 1/4 cup of the olive oil, the garlic, chiles, olives, and cumin seeds, and stir into the flour to form a rough dough. Tip the dough out on to a floured surface and knead until smooth and elastic. Place in a lightly oiled bowl, cover with plastic wrap, and let rise at room temperature for 1–11/2 hours, until almost doubled in size.

Tip out the dough and knead lightly to knock out the air, then roll out to a rectangle about 1/2 inch thick. Cut the rectangle in half diagonally to form 2 triangles. Cover loosely with plastic wrap to prevent a skin forming and let rest for 20 minutes.

Preheat the oven to 400°F. Now lightly stretch the triangles a little by hand or with a rolling pin, maintaining the triangle shape. Dust lightly with flour and then, with a sharp knife, cut 3 or 4 slashes in each triangle, being sure to cut right through the dough.

Line a large baking sheet with wax paper and carefully transfer the triangles to it, stretching them to open out the slashes. Bake for 20 minutes, until golden brown and spongy. Restrain yourself until the fougasse has cooled a little before devouring it!

11/2 lbs. white bread flour (about 6 cups)
1 tablespoon salt
1 envelope of rapid rise yeast
2 cups lukewarm water
1/4 cup, plus 2 tablespoons olive oil
1 garlic clove, crushed
2 serrano chiles, seeded and chopped
1 cup black olives, pitted and
  roughly chopped
2 teaspoons cumin seeds, toasted in a
  dry frying pan

HOT TIP Make the fougasse using spicy olives from a deli and omit the chiles and cumin.

Grilled black pepper nans

Nan is a Punjabi bread, usually baked in tandoor clay ovens to give a wonderful charred flavor. Unfortunately most of us do not have tandoor ovens but the baking can be done in the oven or, as here, under a hot broiler. This recipe is adapted from Linda Collister's wonderful *Bread Book*.

Makes 8

1 teaspoon cracked black peppercorns
  (see Hot Tip on p.28)
2 cups self-rising flour
2 tablespoons Greek yoghurt
  (or thick whole milk yoghurt)
1 teaspoon salt
1 teaspoon ground coriander

Heat a small frying pan over medium heat, add the black pepper, and keep it moving for 20 seconds, until it gives off its peppery fragrance. Remove from the pan and set aside.

Put the flour, yoghurt, and salt in a bowl and add 1/2 cup warm water a little at a time, working it into the flour with your fingers until it forms a slightly sticky dough. Lightly mix in the ground coriander and black pepper. Knead for a few seconds, then cover with a damp cloth and leave at room temperature for 1-11/4 hours.

To cook, preheat the broiler to its highest setting. Flour your hands, pull off small pieces of the dough, and shape each one into a ball. Roll out on a floured surface into an oval shape about 6–8 inches long. Place the nans under the hot broiler until they puff up and char-blister; this shouldn't take more than 40 seconds. Turn them over and cook on the second side, keep them warm while the others cook. Serve warm.

HOT TIP It's worth experimenting with all types of spices for these nans – cumin, fenugreek, turmeric, and nigella, for example.

Quick garlic chili bread

Preheat the broiler to its highest setting. In a blender, blitz together the garlic, harissa, oil, and basil until smooth. Brush a generous amount of this paste over each slice of baguette. Place on a baking tray, sprinkle with the cheese, and place under the broiler until golden and bubbling. Serve hot.

3 garlic cloves, crushed
2 tablespoons Harissa (see p.156)
1/2 cup olive oil
A good handful of basil leaves
1 baguette, cut into slices 1 inch thick
1 tablespoon grated Cheddar cheese

Ground lamb and feta pide

Pide is a sort of Turkish pizza, with a spicy lamb topping rather like a kofta mix. I like to drizzle some yoghurt mixed with grated onion and chopped mint over it just before serving, to temper the heat of the spicy lamb.

Sift the flour and salt into a mixing bowl, make a well in the center and put the potato in it. Put the yeast and sugar in a small bowl, pour on the tepid water, and mix thoroughly until dissolved. Mix the yeast mixture slowly into the potato and flour and then tip out and knead to a soft and pliable dough, adding a little more water if necessary. Place in a lightly oiled bowl, cover with a damp cloth, and let rise at room temperature for 1–11/2 hours.

For the filling, heat the oil in a heavy saucepan, add the ground lamb, and fry until browned all over. Add the onion, chile, and garlic, and cook for 1 minute. Add the tomato paste and spices, and cook for 2 minutes, then stir in 2/3 cup of water. Bring to a boil, then lower the heat and cook for 10-12 minutes, until reduced and thick. Let cool.

Preheat oven to 375°F and place a large baking sheet in it to heat up. Knock back the dough, divide in half, and roll out each piece into a circle about 9 inches in diameter. Brush with the olive oil. Spread the cooled lamb mixture on top, scatter over it the feta cheese, and bake in the oven on the hot baking tray for about 10–12 minutes, until the base is crisp. Serve warm.

a scant 2 cups white bread flour, sifted

1 teaspoon salt

1/3 cup mashed potato (unseasoned)

1 tablespoon fresh yeast

1 teaspoon sugar

1/2 cup lukewarm water

2 tablespoons olive oil

For the filling:

3 tablespoons olive oil

12 ounces lean ground lamb

1 onion, finely chopped

1 small hot chile, seeded and finely chopped

2 garlic cloves, crushed

1 tablespoon tomato paste

1 tablespoon ground coriander

1/2 teaspoon cayenne pepper

1 cup crumbled feta cheese

sauces and spice mixes

✳ Hot lime and chile pickle

This fiery pickle is a staple of Indian cooking. Serve as a dip, with poppadoms, or as an accompaniment to main courses. It is also good mixed with yoghurt and used as a dip for kebabs or vegetables. The flavor is quite tart, so if you prefer a sweeter pickle, add 2 tablespoons of honey.

Makes about 1–11/4 cups

6 limes

1/4 cup sea salt (or Kosher salt)

11/4 cups fresh lemon juice

6 garlic cloves, crushed

4 green chiles, thinly sliced

3 tablespoons ground cumin

2 tablespoons My curry paste (see p.154) or curry powder

1/2 cup sesame oil

Wash the limes, place them in a saucepan with half the salt, and pour in enough water to cover – about 21/2 cups. Bring to a boil, then remove from the heat and let soak for 15 minutes or until the skins are soft. Drain the limes, dry them well, and let cool.

Cut the limes into large pieces, removing the seeds, then sprinkle the rest of the salt over them and mix with all the remaining ingredients. Place in a sterilized jar, seal, and keep for up to 1 week before using. Once opened, the pickle will keep for about a month in the refrigerator.

HOT TIP As a short cut, you could buy lime pickle from an Asian grocery store and spike it with chile.

peppercorn mustard and anchovy mayonnaise

is tangy mayonnaise is good with grilled or deep-fried fish and with fish cakes.

Makes about 1 cup

2 anchovy fillets, rinsed and dried

2 egg yolks

2 tablespoons white wine vinegar

1 tablespoon green peppercorn mustard

2/3 cup olive oil

Salt and freshly ground black pepper

und the anchovy fillets in a mortar or crush them th a fork in a bowl. Add the egg yolks, vinegar, d mustard, and mix together. Gradually whisk in the olive oil, drop by drop at first, to form an emulsion.

Season to taste with salt and pepper.

green peppercorn béarnaise sauce

1/4 cup white wine vinegar

1 small bay leaf

1 teaspoon black peppercorns, lightly cracked (see Hot Tip on p.28)

A few tarragon stalks

2 egg yolks

2 sticks (1 cup) butter, clarified (see Hot Tip)

1 tablespoon lemon juice

A pinch of cayenne pepper

2 ounce can of green peppercorns, drained, rinsed and puréed

Salt

lace the vinegar, bay leaf, peppercorns, and rragon stalks in a small saucepan, simmer until e vinegar is reduced by half, and then strain.

lace egg yolks and the vinegar reduction in a owl set over a pan of simmering water (or in the p of a double boiler), making sure the water does ot touch the bottom of the bowl. Whisk the mixure until it is thick enough to leave a ribbon on the surface when trailed from the whisk. Add the clarified butter a little at a time, whisking continually, until the sauce forms an emulsion. Stir in the lemon juice, season with salt and the cayenne pepper, and fold in the green peppercorn purée. The sauce can be kept warm for up to 2 hours before use as long as it is at the right temperature – I find a vacuum flask ideal for the purpose.

HOT TIP To clarify butter, heat it gently in a small pan until it begins to boil. Boil for 2 minutes, then pour off the clarified butter though a fine conical strainer or a cheesecloth-lined strainer, leaving the white, milky sediment in the pan.

VARIATIONS

Smoky pepper béarnaise Replace the green peppercorns and cayenne with 1 large red pepper, roasted, peeled, and puréed, and 1 teaspoon of smoked paprika.

Chile béarnaise Replace the green peppercorns and cayenne with 1 tablespoon of hot chile sauce.

Mustard béarnaise Replace the green peppercorns and cayenne with 1 tablespoon of whole-grain mustard.

Horseradish béarnaise Replace the green peppercorns and cayenne with 1 tablespoon of grated horseradish.

Hot achiote baste

Achiote seeds come from the annatto tree and are popular in the Yucatan peninsula of Mexico. They have a brick-red color and an earthy flavor. Ready-made achiote paste is available but if you are using seeds you will need to soak them in water overnight and then grind them to a paste. Achiote baste can be brushed on to meat and left to marinate for 1 hour before grilling, then used to baste the meat during cooking.

Place the chiles in a blender with all the dry ingredients and blitz to a paste, adding the liquids a little at a time to form a purée.

Makes about 3/4 cup

3 ancho chiles, roasted (see p.8) and thinly sliced

2 garlic cloves, crushed

1/2 teaspoon ground allspice

1 teaspoon cumin seeds, toasted in a dry frying pan

1 tablespoon achiote paste (or 11/2 teaspoons achiote seeds)

1 tablespoon olive oil

2 tablespoons white wine vinegar

6 tablespoons fresh orange juice

✳ Mexican chile sauce

Serve this classic Mexican sauce with rolled tortillas or stir it into rice dishes and soups.

Put the roasted ancho and guajillo chiles in a pan, pour in enough boiling water to cover them, and simmer for 5 minutes. Remove from the heat and let soak for about 30 minutes, until soft. Drain the chiles, reserving the soaking liquid, and put them in a blender with half the liquid. Add the chicken stock or water, garlic, cumin seeds, and cloves, and blend until smooth. Season with salt, then finish with the lime juice. Store in the fridge, where it will keep for 1 week.

Makes about 2 cups

4 ancho chiles, roasted (see p.8)

4 guajillo chiles, roasted (see p.8)

1 cup chicken stock or water

4 garlic cloves, chopped

1/4 teaspoon cumin seeds

2 cloves

Juice of 1 lime

Salt

horseradish sauce

This is very easy to make and so much better than commercial horseradish sauce. Besides having it with your Sunday roast, you could try it with Italian charcuterie or smoked fish such as trout, mackerel, and eel. It also makes a good topping for beet soup, mixed with a little yoghurt.

Lightly whip the cream until it begins to thicken enough to hang from the whisk without dropping. Gently fold in the crème fraîche, horseradish, wine vinegar, and mustard, then season to taste. Add the chives, if using. Refrigerate until ready to serve.

Makes about 11/4 cups

6 tablespoons heavy cream

1/4 cup crème fraîche

3 tablespoons grated horseradish root

1 tablespoon white wine vinegar

1 teaspoon Dijon mustard

2 tablespoons chopped chives (optional)

Salt and freshly ground black pepper

The classic American cocktail sauce
(hot tomato and horseradish)

This is nothing like the British cocktail sauce. It has a terrific flavor and really livens up seafood such as lobster and shrimp. It also makes a good dip for vegetables.

Mix all of the ingredients together in a bowl, adding salt and pepper to taste. The sauce can be kept in the fridge for about a week but will lose its freshness after a couple of days.

Makes 11/4 cups

11/4 cups tomato ketchup

2 tablespoons grated horseradish root

1 garlic clove, crushed

3 tablespoons lemon juice

3 drops of Tabasco sauce

Salt and freshly ground black pepper

Asian sweet chile sauce

Place all the ingredients in a food processor and blend until the texture is fine. Store in the fridge. It will keep for up to 1 month, or longer if you bottle it in a sterilized jar.

Makes about 11/4 cups

21/4 lbs. red serrano chiles, stems removed

2 inch piece of fresh ginger root, chopped

2 garlic cloves, crushed

2 teaspoons rice wine vinegar

1 tablespoon sugar

2 teaspoons lime juice

Chile jelly

This makes an excellent accompaniment to cold meats. I also like it brushed over chicken during roasting for a wonderfully hot, sweet, and sticky glaze.

Gently heat the red currant jelly in a pan until dissolved. In a blender, blitz together all the remaining ingredients and then add to the jelly. Bring to a boil, reduce the heat, and cook for about 30 minutes, until the jelly is thick and syrupy. Transfer to a bowl and let cool.

This may be kept in a covered container for up to one month in the fridge.

a heaped cup red currant jelly
(or, if unavailable, use cranberry jelly)
1 habanero chile, seeded and chopped
1 red pepper, chopped
Juice of 1 lemon
2 drops of Tabasco sauce
2 tablespoons cider vinegar

Chile and raisin jam

Depending on the strength of the chiles you use, this varies from hot to extremely hot! Serve as a dip for oriental-style dishes such as egg rolls or tempura. It also makes an excellent burger relish and can be cooked with vegetables, like the Sweet and sour baby onions on page 92.

Put the vinegar and sugar in a small pan and bring to a boil. Add the raisins and cook to a light caramel; the liquid should be syrupy. Stir in the shallots, chiles, ginger, garlic, and fish sauce, then remove from the heat and let cool slightly. Place in a blender and blitz to a coarse purée.

Makes about 2 1/2 cups

1 cup rice vinegar
a heaped 1/2 cup soft brown sugar
a heaped 1/2 cup raisins
4 shallots, finely chopped
1 lb. red serrano chiles, seeded and chopped
1 tablespoon finely chopped fresh ginger root
2 garlic cloves, crushed
1 teaspoon nam pla (Thai fish sauce)

✳ Chile sambal

This makes a great dip for deep-fried fish and meat. It is also good added to stir-fries to enliven the flavors.

Seed and slice the chiles. Gently heat the oil in a frying pan, add the shallots and garlic, and cook until softened. Add the chiles and cook for 5 minutes, then stir in the tomatoes, sugar, nam pla, and 1/2 cup of water. Cook over medium heat for 10 minutes, then stir in the lime juice. Purée in a blender and season to taste with salt. Let cool, then store in the refrigerator in a sealed container. It will keep for up to a week, longer if bottled in a sterilized jar.

HOT TIP To sterilize jars, wash them thoroughly in hot soapy water, then rinse well and place on a baking tray. Dry in an oven preheated to 275°F.

Makes about 1 1/4 cups

8 large red Thai chiles
2 tablespoons vegetable oil
5 shallots, thinly sliced
4 garlic cloves, sliced
2 tomatoes, skinned, cut into wedges and seeded
1 tablespoon brown sugar
1 teaspoon nam pla (Thai fish sauce)
2 teaspoons lime juice
Salt

Jalapeño and green tomato salsa

This is a good all-purpose salsa. Try it with grilled fish or seafood, kebabs, or classic Mexican dishes such as tacos and fajitas.

Combine all the ingredients in a bowl, adding salt and pepper to taste.

Let marinate for 1 hour before using, to let the flavors meld.

l lb. green tomatoes, seeded and chopped

4 scallions, finely shredded

6 tablespoons chopped cilantro

2 jalapeño chiles, seeded and chopped

1 garlic clove, crushed

Juice of 2 limes

2 tablespoons maple syrup

Salt and freshly ground black pepper

ot Mexican salsa

ntly heat the oil in a pan, add the garlic, onion, d chiles, then remove from the heat and let cool. **ir** in all the remaining ingredients. Let marinate

for at least 2 hours before using, to let the flavors meld.

2 tablespoons vegetable oil

3 garlic cloves, crushed

1 onion, finely chopped

1 habanero chile, seeded and finely chopped

2 jalapeño chiles, seeded and finely chopped

1 lb. plum tomatoes, cut into 1/2 inch dice

Juice of 2 limes

1/2 teaspoon dried oregano or 1 tablespoon fresh oregano

2 tablespoons maple syrup or honey

A pinch each of ground cumin and salt

1/4 cup chopped cilantro

aribbean mojo

e habanero chile gives this fruity salsa a powerful bite. Serve with grilled fish or meat. I particularly like with tuna burgers or grilled lobster.

ace the diced mango, pineapple, and avocado a bowl, then mix in the lime and orange juice, antro, sugar, chile, and scallions.

Season with salt and feshly ground black pepper. Cover and let stand for about 30 minutes before using.

1 mango, peeled, pitted, and cut into 1/4 inch dice

2 ounces pineapple (about 11/2 rings), cut into 1/4 inch dice

1 avocado, peeled, pitted, and cut into 1/4 inch dice

Juice of 2 limes

1/4 cup orange juice

2 tablespoons chopped cilantro

A pinch of sugar

1 habanero chile, seeded and finely diced

4 scallions, shredded

Salt and freshly ground black pepper

* Aromatic chili oil

Chili oil can be stored indefinitely in a cool, dry place, away from direct sunlight. However, I prefer to use it within four months, otherwise the flavor begins to lose its freshness. It is wonderful in all types of dishes, such as dressings, soups, and salads, and to spice up sauces and stir-fries. Below is my simple recipe for chili oil, together with a few variations on the theme from around the world.

Makes about 21/2 cups

4 jalapeño or serrano chiles
21/2 cups vegetable or peanut oil

Cut the chiles in half to expose the seeds (if you prefer a milder oil, leave the chiles whole). Gently heat the oil in a pan, then add the chiles. Leave over medium heat for about 5–10 minutes, then remove from the heat and let infuse overnight in the pan.

The next day, remove the chiles from the oil, strain the oil into sterilized bottles, and seal.

HOT TIP If, like me, you prefer the oil to have a real kick, leave the chiles in it when bottling.

VARIATIONS

South American chili oil Replace the chiles with 1 shredded habanero chile. Add 1 tablespoon of fresh oregano, 1/2 teaspoon of allspice, 2 garlic cloves, peeled, and 1 bay leaf.

Indian chili oil Add 1 tablespoon each of roasted cumin seeds, fenugreek, black mustard seeds, and crushed cardamom seeds.

Oriental chili oil Add 11/2 teaspoons of toasted Szechuan peppercorns, 2 star anise, and 1/4 cup of sesame oil.

Smoky guacamole en molcajete with chili oil

Molcajete is the Mexican name for a mortar and pestle, which is used to make the guacamole. Serve as a dip for crudités, rolled up in tortillas, or as an accompaniment to poached salmon.

Put the roasted chipotle chile in a bowl, cover with hot water, and let soak for 30 minutes. Drain and chop finely.

Cut the avocado in half, remove the pit, and peel off the skin. Cut each half in half again. Heat a ridged grill pan (or, better still, a barbecue grill), brush the avocado wedges with the olive oil, and grill on both sides until they are lightly browned but not heated through; do not let them brown too much or they will be bitter. Let cool.

Crush the garlic in a mortar and pestle, pressing on it to release as much juice as possible. Add the avocado and crush with the garlic. Then add the chopped chipotle chile, onion, and cilantro. Finally, mix in the lime juice and the pomegranate seeds, if using, then season with salt and pepper. Transfer to a serving dish, pour the chili oil on top and serve.

1/2 chipotle chile, roasted (see p.8)

1 firm but ripe avocado

1 tablespoon olive oil

1 garlic clove, peeled

1 onion, finely chopped

1 tablespoon chopped cilantro

Juice of 1 lime

Seeds from 1 pomegranate (optional)

2 tablespoons South American chili oil (see p.152)

Salt and freshly ground black pepper

My curry paste

Heat a large frying pan over high heat. When hot, add all the whole spices and toast, shaking the pan frequently, until they begin to give off a rich aroma. Remove from the pan and let cool.

Grind the toasted spices in a spice mill or coffee grinder – or in a mortar and pestle – and mix in the ginger, turmeric, and cognac. Place in a bowl and stir in the oil to form a thick paste. This should keep for about a month in the fridge, although I always find I use it up pretty quickly.

Makes about 3/4 cup

2 tablespoons coriander seeds

2 tablespoons fennel seeds

1 tablespoon cardamom pods

1 tablespoon black peppercorns

2 teaspoons cumin seeds

1 teaspoon fenugreek seeds

1 teaspoon black mustard seeds

1 cinnamon stick

5 cloves

1 teaspoon ground ginger

1 tablespoon ground turmeric

2 teaspoons cayenne pepper

About 2 tablespoons vegetable oil

* Ethiopian berbere

Place the roasted chiles in a bowl, pour over them 1¼ cups of boiling water and let soak for 30 minutes. Meanwhile, heat a heavy frying pan, add the peppercorns and cumin seeds, and toss them over medium heat until they become fragrant.

Drain the chiles, reserving the soaking liquid, and place them in a blender. Add the grated onion, garlic, and ground spices, as well as the toasted peppercorns and cumin seeds. Add a little of the chile soaking liquid and blitz to a smooth paste, then add the oil and blitz again.

Place the mixture in a small pan and cook over low heat for 10 minutes, stirring frequently so it doesn't burn. Remove from the heat and set aside to cool. Transfer the berbere to an airtight container, seal well, and store in the refrigerator for up to 2 weeks.

HOT TIP If you want a slightly milder sauce, remove the seeds from the chiles.

Makes about 2/3 cup

1 ounce dried red chiles (around 6-8 chiles), such as ancho or De Arbol, roasted (see p.8)

1 teaspoon black peppercorns

2 teaspoons cumin seeds

1 onion, grated

2 garlic cloves, crushed

1 teaspoon ground cardamom

1/4 teaspoon ground allspice

1/4 teaspoon ground cinnamon

1/2 teaspoon ground coriander

1/2 teaspoon ground ginger

2 tablespoons smoked paprika

3 tablespoons peanut oil

Green Thai curry paste

Heat a heavy frying pan over low heat, add the coriander seeds, cumin seeds, and aniseed, and toast for 2 minutes, until they give off their aroma. Transfer to a spice mill or coffee grinder and blitz to a fine powder.

Put all the rest of the ingredients except the shrimp paste in a blender and blitz. Add the ground spices and shrimp paste and blitz again to a smooth paste. Store in an airtight container in the fridge, where it should keep for about a month.

VARIATION

Red Thai curry paste Prepare as above but substitute 6 red serrano or jalapeño chiles for the green chiles, increase the garlic to 8 cloves, and use 12 black peppercorns instead of 1/8 teaspoon. Add 3 tablespoons of vegetable oil with the shrimp paste.

Makes about 1 cup

1 tablespoon coriander seeds

1 teaspoon cumin seeds

1 teaspoon whole aniseed

12 green bird's eye or Thai chiles, chopped

2 shallots, chopped

3 garlic cloves, crushed

1 inch piece of fresh galangal, peeled and chopped

2 lemongrass sticks, outer layers removed, chopped

8 kaffir lime leaves

1 tablespoon cilantro, stalks and roots only

1/2 teaspoon black peppercorns

2 teaspoons blachan (dried shrimp paste)

* Harissa

Heat the oil in a large, heavy pan. Add all the ingredients except the salt and pepper and cook over medium heat for about 5 minutes or until the red pepper has softened. Add 1¼ cups of water and bring to a boil. Reduce the heat and simmer gently for 10 minutes or until the pepper is really soft. Purée in a blender until smooth. Season to taste with salt and pepper and let cool. This will keep in the fridge for 10 days or in the freezer for 1 month.

1 tablespoon vegetable oil

1 large red pepper, finely chopped

3 red chiles, seeded and chopped

2 garlic cloves, crushed

1 tablespoon ground coriander

1 tablespoon ground cumin

1 tablespoon ground caraway

2 tablespoons tomato paste

Salt and freshly ground black pepper

Asian blackened spice mix

This is an adaptation of the classic Creole-Cajun spice mix – an idea I had one day when I wanted to prepare a spicy Asian-style fish dish. Flavored with cardamom and fennel seeds, it is great with meat as well as fish.

Heat a heavy frying pan over high heat, then add the whole spices and toast them, shaking the pan frequently, until they begin to give off a rich aroma. Place the toasted spices in a spice mill or coffee grinder, add the turmeric, cayenne, and ginger, and blitz to a powder. (If you have time on your hands you could pound them in a mortar and pestle instead.) Store in an airtight container.

2 tablespoons coriander seeds

2 tablespoons fennel seeds

1 tablespoon cardamom pods

1 tablespoon black peppercorns

2 teaspoons cumin seeds

1 teaspoon fenugreek seeds

1 teaspoon black mustard seeds

5 cloves

1 cinnamon stick

1 tablespoon ground turmeric

2 teaspoons cayenne pepper

1 teaspoon ground ginger

Colombo spice mix

This Sri Lankan curry powder is made with roasted basmati rice, which may sound unusual but gives it a wonderful nutty flavor.

Heat a heavy frying pan over medium heat, add the rice, and toast for 3–4 minutes, until golden. Transfer to a bowl. Put the whole spices in the pan for 3–4 minutes, shaking the pan frequently, until lightly toasted and fragrant. Add the spices to the rice and let cool. Blitz the mixture to a fine powder in a spice mill or coffee grinder, then add the turmeric. Store in an airtight container.

1/2 cup basmati rice

6 tablespoons cumin seeds

1/2 cup coriander seeds

2 tablespoons black mustard seeds

2 tablespoons black peppercorns

2 tablespoons fenugreek seeds

2 teaspoons whole cloves

1/2 cup ground turmeric

Blackened Cajun spice mix

A punchy spice mix that originates from Louisiana and is used extensively in Cajun and Creole cooking. It is very adaptable and can be added to all sorts of fish and meat dishes.

Place all the ingredients in a spice mill or coffee grinder and blitz to a fine powder. Transfer the spice mix to an airtight container and seal well before storing.

1 tablespoon salt

1 tablespoon hot paprika

1 teaspoon garlic powder

1 teaspoon black peppercorns

1 teaspoon chili powder (or cayenne pepper)

1 tablespoon dried thyme

1 tablespoon dried oregano

2 teaspoons ground cumin

Sri Lankan spice mix

The coriander, cumin, fennel seeds, and fenugreek need to be dry-roasted separately, as they tend to darken at different stages: heat a small, heavy frying pan, add each spice and, shaking the pan frequently, roast until the seeds darken slightly and begin to give off their aroma. Transfer to a plate and set aside.

Put all the remaining ingredients in the pan and dry-roast for about 30 seconds, until they give off a rich aroma. Place all the ingredients in a spice mill or coffee grinder and blitz to a fine powder. Store in an airtight container.

6 tablespoons coriander seeds

3 tablespoons cumin seeds

1 tablespoon fennel seeds

1 teaspoon fenugreek seeds

2 teaspoons chili powder

2 teaspoons ground cinnamon

1 teaspoon cloves

5 dried curry leaves

10 cardamom pods

Barbecue spice mix

This adaptable spice mix can be sprinkled over vegetables or rubbed on fish or meat before barbecuing or broiling. Like all spice mixes, it keeps well in an airtight container for about a month but the flavor will gradually deteriorate if it is stored much longer than this.

Put all of the ingredients in a bowl and mix until thoroughly combined. Transfer to an airtight container and seal well before storing.

1/4 cup dried red chili flakes

3 tablespoons paprika

1 tablespoon ground cumin

1 tablespoon ground coriander

1 tablespoon sugar

2 teaspoons salt

1 teaspoon mustard powder

1 teaspoon freshly ground black pepper

1 teaspoon dried thyme

1 teaspoon mild curry powder

2 teaspoons cayenne pepper

Index

Acknowledgments

During the writing of this book, there have been many people whose help, encouragement and enthusiasm has been invaluable.

My very grateful thanks go to:

Linda Tubby for preparing and styling the food shots for photography and for making the dishes look delicious.

Jane Middleton for her usual superb editing of my recipes. She is simply "The Best".

Gus Filgate, friend and truly exceptional photographer.

Róisín Nield for sourcing such wonderful props.

Vanessa Courtier for her beautiful design.

Fiona Lindsay and Linda Shanks, my agents, for just about everything.

Lara King for her endless hours typing the manuscript.

Michael and Joy Michaud for their help, friendship, and for providing some truly wonderful fresh chiles for photography. (Peppers by Post: Sea Spring Farm, West Bexington, Dorchester, Dorset, Tel: 01308 897892).

The Cool Chilli Company for providing some fantastic dried and powdered chile varieties (PO Box 5702, London W11 2ES, Tel: 0207 229 9360).

Geoffrey Gelardi, Managing Director, and my dedicated kitchen brigade, especially Justin Woods, Christophe Poupardin, and Samantha Mills, for helping with photographic preparations, especially during busy times.

Finally a huge thank you to Kyle Cathie, and her dedicated team, especially Sheila Boniface for all the hard work, support, and friendship, and for believing that this book might be a "hot" idea to publish.

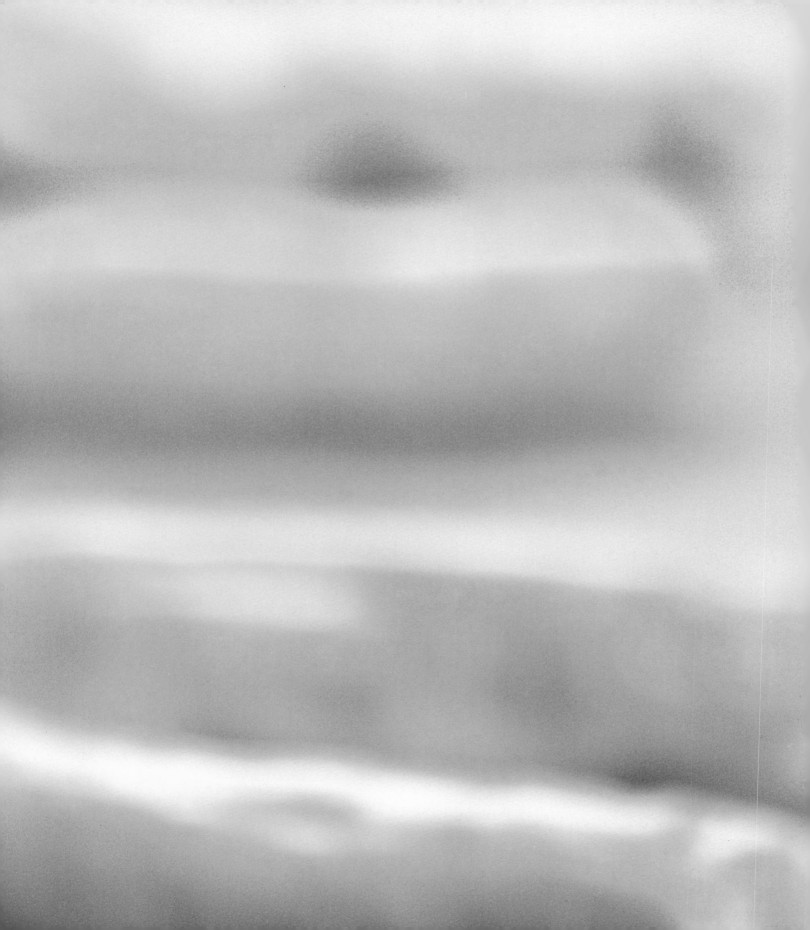